ASYLUM

A MEMOIR & MANIFESTO

EDAFE OKPORO

SIMON & SCHUSTER

New York London Toronto Sydney New Delhi

Simon & Schuster
1230 Avenue of the Americas
New York, NY 10020

Some names have been changed.

First Simon & Schuster hardcover edition June 2022

For information about special discounts for bulk purchases, please contact Simon & Schuster Special Sales at 1-866-506-1949 or business@simonandschuster.com.

The Simon & Schuster Speakers Bureau can bring authors to your live event. For more information or to book an event, contact the Simon & Schuster Speakers Bureau at 1-866-248-3049 or visit our website at www.simonspeakers.com.

Interior design by Kyle Kabel

Manufactured in the United States of America

1 3 5 7 9 10 8 6 4 2

Library of Congress Cataloging-in-Publication Data has been applied for.

ISBN 978-1-9821-8374-5
ISBN 978-1-9821-8376-9 (ebook)

To the women in my life:
my mother, Mrs. Igho Akanusi;
my grandmother, Mrs. Alice Akanusi;
and my aunt, Mrs. Grace Erhimona.
Thank you for raising me.

Contents

ASYLUM

Prologue

Market day, as it's popularly known, happened once a year in my part of Nigeria.

Market day had been a tradition long before the invention of paper currency. My parents told me that trade by bartering was the only form of exchange. Most families in Southern Nigeria had a small farm where they grew fruits and vegetables to sustain their families. The small farm in their backyard sometimes sustained them—otherwise, families would have to manage their harvests and bring them to the market to barter for the food and wares they could not grow or make themselves.

On market day, there would be a mixture of regular local market shops and farmers with rice or cassava, who would exchange with fishermen or livestock farmers. Palm oil producers could exchange with those who had yams. Women might trade clothes and clay pots for food. Many did not have shops or storefronts, but instead sold their produce on the floor, which they covered with a cloth sack, or from plates balanced atop their heads.

If you had woken up next to me as a child on market day, you would have been annoyed by my excitement. I always looked forward to going with my mother to the popular Igbudu Market. The sights and sounds were like stepping into an amusement park. Though usually market day was not meant for boys to attend—in Warri, where I was raised, mostly mothers and their young girls would go. The boys had no patience for their mothers, going over each item's price, hopping from shop to shop, sharing in conversation with the other women at day's end. For Warri boys, going to the market meant acting like a woman—they would brag about refusing to help their mothers. But not me—I was the only child living in my parents' home at the time, so my mother always took me to the market with her, which I secretly delighted in.

Spring ushers in the rainy season to Warri, bringing with it looming clouds and almost daily precipitation that turned the sand beneath our feet mushy and claylike. Nevertheless, this was my favorite time of year, for it meant the beginning of crab season. I loved to watch the live crabs in their baskets as the traders tried to tame and settle them. But this season also meant my mum would get us some crab at the market for stew.

We would walk around the market for about three hours on a good day, and when my mother was in her element, we spent the whole day in the market picking up raw foods or new clothes. When we were done shopping, I could see her face grow tired and weary, but she would always flash me a smile, as if to say *it's okay.* The bounty was typically too much for my mother to carry, and I was still a small child then. Though boys wouldn't go to the market with their own mothers, some of the older ones would linger on the outskirts, trying to make a hustle by helping the women carry their goods to a taxi for a small reward.

I remember one day, after we had spent hours going line by line picking items, my mother said it was time to go home to prepare the crab stew before my dad got too hungry. We waited for the boys to come pick up our goods and bring them to the taxi line. Two bald boys with muscular chests, one shirtless and the other in a wifebeater, approached us with sun-slick foreheads, sweat mingling with the foul stench of labor. When they got to us, they began arguing about who would help us in order to secure a tip. Quickly, they turned aggressive, beginning to push each other, and I could feel the muddy floor beneath us thumping. Despite their fighting, no one tried to break them up—this was quite normal, apparently, to everyone except me.

One of them shouted at the other, "You know me? I be Jaguda!" in pidgin English. He smacked his chest, and it sounded like a clap of thunder striking his torso. "I'm a troublemaker," he stressed.

They held each other tightly as they struggled, sweat dripping around them into the mud. I found myself sweating suddenly too, from unease. What was I supposed to do? Was I meant to get involved? Protect my small mother? Instead, I crumpled to the floor of the market and shielded myself from them. I felt my mother's sweeping, printed dress glide down next to me as she took me between her legs, held me safe and close. She tapped my head slowly, hoping to calm me.

"It is okay, my son," she said. "This is how Warri boys are supposed to behave."

Their fight was triggering, but my mother's acceptance of it was even more troubling. In my mother's soothing, I found calm and terror at the same time. This was just one of many times I found myself stuck in the parade of masculinity and intimidation that was so common for Warri boys, but that I could not bring myself to be a part of. Beyond this market, my inability to "act" like a real Warri boy would become a constant struggle. Over the years, it would lead to disapproval from my family, my close friends, and the community in which I was raised. At times, I would find it not only difficult, but life-threatening. I would be mocked for carrying unisex bags to class. I would be ostracized by my father and other men in Warri, and at school. Ultimately, I would be attacked by a violent mob—not just for being an untrue Warri boy, but for being a gay man.

This battle with masculinity—with accepting myself and who I am—would eventually lead me to flee the only home and family I had ever known and ever loved. But what waited for me on the other side were challenges I could have never imagined—along with the promise of freedom.

CHAPTER ONE

Growing Up (and Coming Out) in Nigeria

When I was nine years old, my teacher asked me to join the debate team. "Why me?" I asked. I knew being the only boy on our class's debate team would put a target on my back—that it would only uphold my classmates' belief that I was too feminine. So I continued to refuse my teacher's proposition to join, while my teacher continued to enumerate reasons why I should: "Edafe, you argue with your classmates all the time." She saw in me, early on, a quality I would not come to recognize in myself for many years: a conviction in my beliefs.

My closest friend in primary school was a girl named Gloria—we sat close to each other in class and tried to answer most of our teacher's questions. "Gloria and Edafe," our teacher sometimes remarked when surveying the room, "this question is not for you."

Gloria and I would walk home from school together, along with my elder sister Anita. My mum and dad sometimes sat in front of our veranda when Gloria and I passed by. Once, my mum pronounced to us, "Edafe, Gloria will be a good wife for you!" while I tried to hide the embarrassment coloring my face.

My father, on the other hand, is what you might consider a traditionalist. He believed that men were the heads of households, and he viewed marriage as an arrangement between parents for the children rather than something you did for love. He never understood why I was so close to Gloria; instead, he suggested I should concentrate on my education and spend time with the boys at school. Yet Gloria and some of the other girls in my class were the only people I could relate to. And Gloria was the only one of my friends who had the courage to stand up to our classmates when they would call me a "mama's boy" or when the other boys accused me of behaving like a woman. In Nigeria, gender stereotypes and roles were strongly adhered to—a boy who was close to girls in the classroom and spent a lot of time with his mother was an atypical picture of masculinity. I wasn't brave enough to tell my dad or anyone else that I was being bullied by the boys in my class. I worried he would only see this as a weakness, a flaw—that I wouldn't grow up to be a true African man who could accept responsibilities and care for his family.

I knew that being the only boy on the debate team would make things harder for me, but I convinced myself that my classmates' mockery came from a place of jealousy. They would have loved to be in a position of representing the class; however, they would never do so at the expense of their egos. Yet Gloria kept remarking how nice it would be for us to compete together. So, for her, I finally agreed to join.

Our class was made up of about sixteen people, and when class was over, the debate team waited behind for practice. The team was made up of four people: three girls and me. We were put into pairs—Gloria and I were partners—and our teacher told us she hoped we would not fail her. "No, Ma," we'd replied. For months we practiced each day after school, debating topics such as the history of Nigeria, world leaders, geography, and government's role in society. Our teachers chose topics that were controversial, but they abstained from politics. The goal of the debate was to build our confidence and give us a working knowledge of the world. But the best part of the debate team was that it would leave me with an invaluable skill—it gave us an edge in arguing for or against a point of view.

A week before the final debate competition was hosted at our school, we had a primary debate practice in class. It took the form of the actual debate set: our chairs were turned to face each other, with Gloria and I on one side, and the other two girls—Amaka and Faith—facing us. Our teacher sat in the middle, and the rest of the class was our audience. With our classmates in attendance, I felt an immense pressure to succeed—if I failed to debate well against one of the girls, the boys would certainly ridicule me.

The debate, which was more of a combination of debating and quizzing, had three sections, the first of which was in the form of a spelling bee, using English spellings; this was Gloria's domain. The second round was world countries and capitals, my strong suit. After two rounds, though, Amaka's group was leading. I had failed spelling two country's names; I could hear boys in the class whispering already. Yet I tried to remain confident.

The third round was world politics and was structured as a debate. This was where Gloria and I stole the game. Our teacher asked, "Is Nigeria currently an OPEC state?" We buzzed quickly and answered with a confident *yes*. To my surprise, the audience roared when Gloria and I ascended. The class jumped out of their seats, chanting, "Edafe and Gloria! Edafe and Gloria!" Winning this trial meant Gloria and I would represent our school at the state finals. We might even be on the local news. This was a big deal.

I should have been afraid, but I no longer was. I felt only courage as Gloria and I continued to prepare for the quiz portion.

"Edafe," she'd say in her singsong voice. "Tell me: What is the capital of Morocco?" Was it Casablanca? It must be, I thought. Gloria laughed. "No," she said, smiling with dimples and flashing the gap between her front teeth. "Wrong answer."

"So, tell me, what is the right answer?" I protested.

"I will not," she said, and jolted into a laughing run. I chased after her until I'd finally caught her, both of us falling and panting on the ground.

"Okay, okay," she said. "It is Rabat!"

I tried to argue with her—I was sure it wasn't Rabat—but of course Gloria was right. She had a charm, a welcoming smile that made her never seem boastful of her competencies. I continued arguing with her over the correct answer on our walk home. By the time we arrived at my house, I was willing to admit she was right.

Weeks later, the final tournament took place in our school's assembly hall—this was no longer an intimate class affair. More than one hundred students, teachers, and parents—though only my sister Anita was able to attend—filed into the hall as we heard the announcer's boom from the prep room: "The final competition is here!" We were called to the stage, waiting behind the curtains for our moment. The urge to win coursed through me—my hands were sweating, my legs shook. It was then that I felt Gloria tap me and say, "Stop being afraid," and wrapped her hand around my thumb. I could feel my fear morphing into something else: excitement.

We walked onto the stage to a roar of cheers from our classmates and peers, and took our places. We debated topics such as how Nigeria gained independence from Britain, and whether colonizers should have stayed longer. Should we adopt the UK prime minister and monarchy system of government or a democratic system? Though the debate lasted much longer, it felt as though it went by in a blink. The other two teams were more experienced, sharper and faster with their arguments. Unfortunately, Gloria and I lost, coming in third. We realized that our teacher had not prepped us properly for this kind of argument-style debate as much as she had for a spelling competition.

But any worries I had about being teased for debating with the girls were quickly dispelled—it turns out my mates were proud of me for representing the boys in the class. Afterward, our teacher led us to a cozy reception where our classmates waited. They stood and cheered for me and Gloria when we walked in, treating us as if we'd won. I locked eyes with my sister Anita, who beamed at me with pride. Though when I arrived back home, I was met by my father on our veranda, wearing a solemn face—after all, we had still lost.

* * *

I grew up in Warri, a city in the Southern region of Nigeria. We referred to ourselves as "Waffairians." We had our own lingua franca called pidgin English, which was a mix of English, Portuguese, and many other languages. Your mastery of pidgin English must be backed by bravado and guts. It was about a certain type of swagger. Men were fascinated with the Warri boy's lifestyle, which was ascribed to people who used slang and did things in a certain way.

For instance, a true Warri boy does not back down from a fight or challenge. If someone pushed your chest, challenging you to a fight, people might chant, "You know who I be?" This was a way of asking the challenger to back down or face the pedigree of your street worth. Or they might just say, "You dey craze?" Which simply meant you were crazy to challenge a fight. If the person refused to back down, the challenger might have had to break a bottle with their head to show their strength.

These were the outrageous displays of masculinity that colored my boyhood. I wasn't a true Warri boy. I did not engage in shows of strength; I did not use or relate to the slang. My dad, however, was a real Warri man. If we ran out of matches to light our stove, I'd suggest we ask our neighbors for a matchbox, but my father would refuse. He would rather be hungry than be seen as a man unable to care for his family. To him, masculinity meant not showing any form of weakness to anyone; not having a matchbox meant he was unable to be the man of the house. I remember the lyrics of the song "Gentleman" by Fela, about how being an "Africa man original" was more important than being a gentleman. Men should carry the weight of the home. Though there were strong religious overtones in our perceptions of male and female roles: a man could get married to more than one woman, as women were considered helpers to men. Fela himself married more than twenty wives. To stray from these perceived ideologies of what makes an ideal man was to question the foundations of our traditional African belief in the role of a man and a woman. These were part of the reason my dad was not happy I was so close to Gloria; he sensed I wasn't being an "Africa man original."

Where my father exemplified Nigerian norms for masculinity, my mother bucked tradition. I grew up the youngest of four children, with one older brother and two older sisters. Before I was born, she had two other children who died at age two due to illness; three years after my birth, my mother tried to give birth to another baby—my younger brother—who died at birth, too. I would remain her last born child. In turn, she was very protective of me. In Warri, parents live by the notion of sparing the rod spoiling the child. They believe beating a child is a way to keep them in check. Yet my mother never let anyone lay their hands on me. Instead, she motivated me to study hard and succeed; she bought me gifts such as a new lunch bag to encourage my successes in school.

Maybe my mother's spoiling was to blame, but I had always liked being around women. My parents were not literate but worked full-time, so my dad's younger sister, my aunt—Mrs. Erhimona—attended all school events and functions. She was a well-respected woman—the first person with a college degree in my extended family—who lectured at the petroleum training institute in Warri, which was one of the only petroleum institutions in West Africa. At home, when I wasn't with my mother or my aunt, I had my two older sisters. My elder brother was eleven years older than me; we were not that close, and often the only people I could rely on growing up were my two sisters. I remember afternoons playing with Anita and her dolls, braiding their hair together and painting their faces. This was not, of course, how little Warri boys should spend their playtime. Around Nigeria, little boys were either working the farms with their fathers or in the workshop learning how to make money and provide for their future family.

My father was uncomfortable seeing me play with women all the time. "When will he start playing with the boys?" he would ask my mum. I used to enjoy playing soccer, but the boys' chiding remarks made me dislike attending practice. "You play like a woman," they would say, laughing at me. "You must enjoy touching all the girls you play with." They would tease me and suggest I join the girls' team instead, or that I wasn't man enough to date women. Not playing soccer—something I loved—became an act of self-preservation.

I did not know then what it meant to be gay. I would not come to understand this part of myself for years. But I believe my father sensed my closeness to my mother, sisters, and other girls was a sign of me being different. However, I don't think he understood that his son was gay, because he could not accept the notion that someone can be gay.

Our home was often unstable. When I was ten years old, my father was having financial troubles; he did not have a formal education; he could not get a job for the government, which pays a better salary; and he was involved in gambling. As a result of this hardship, we had to downsize to enable him to care for his family. He lost one of his most precious assets, his Toyota four-wheel-drive car, and could barely afford to feed our family or pay for our school fees. My mother was a full-time housewife for many years, and she had just started her new business selling drinks at a beer parlor. She had to bring in money to support my dad, who had been the breadwinner of the family. There is a lot of stigma surrounding a woman running this sort of business; my mother was public-facing to unmarried and married men who would wind up drunk at her beer parlor at night, but we were all dependent on my father, who could no longer care for the entire family.

A few months into this financial crisis, my elder brother Obatarhe got admitted to Delta State University but could not pursue his education because we could not afford to send him to college and feed the family. So he joined my mother's business and offered more protection for my mother at night. The business was growing, and there was an opportunity for him to become the head of it if it flourished. My brother experienced some cash flow during his time co-running my mother's business and his girlfriend at this time became pregnant. No higher education for him—he would become a dad in his early twenties. He eventually got married, leaving our house for good. My eldest sister, Ovoke, left for Ghana to live with her then boyfriend and now husband, Emmanuel, not long after; and when Anita became pregnant as a teenager, my father banished her from his house. Anita moved in with her boyfriend. Outside our home, Warri itself was riddled with fear of gang violence and wars between the major tribes. For a few more years before I would leave home, it was just me, my dad, and my mum. Mum would always say I was their only hope left of having a child that would go to college.

There is an African belief that a child is shaped by community; we are not solely the responsibility of our parents alone. This, the idea of needing to "man up," and to further my education, were the reasons I was sent away at twelve to live with Mrs. Erhimona—my father's youngest sister—and her husband. She was a devoted Christian, an educated lady, but had no children of her own at this time, only a stepson. My parents believed she could dedicate her time to care for me and give me an opportunity for a better life beyond our broken home and troubled city. Even my overly protective mum knew this was the right decision. There was no future for me in Warri. In the news, there had been reported incidents of a militia group from the Niger Delta who were kidnapping foreign government officials and large corporate employees. They were already recruiting boys my age. It would be hard to leave Gloria behind, but we all knew this was an opportunity I had to take, like it or not. An opportunity to a brighter future, with the God-fearing Mrs. Erhimona.

Mrs. Erhimona was a short, chubby lady with a broad smile and an unrestrained laugh—she reminded me of my mother, empathetic and caring. At that age, I trusted her judgment—that the choices she made for me would steer me toward the right direction of holy uprightness. As a Nigerian woman, born in an era with almost no women earning an education, she graduated top of her class, studying industrial chemistry at the University of Benin. She was a pioneer, an idol. I wanted to be like her in every virtue she displayed as a religious person, an educated woman, and a pseudo mother.

My aunt had made some preparation for my arrival. Mrs. Erhimona was living with her husband and her stepson in a three-bedroom apartment. For the first time, I would share a room with only one other person, and I would have access to a private bathroom—which was not what I grew up with: back home with my parents we had a communal bathroom, which can expose someone to communicable diseases, so this was a step up for me—and a big living room, also an upgrade for me and another reason why I would trade any freedom I would have for this opportunity. In exchange for these accommodations, I would have to attend Sunday Bible study, religious services, and evening group meetings with her. She took her religious events seriously, and as a result, the church became a bigger part of my community as well. At the close of each service at St. Andrew's Cathedral in Warri, she would hang out with her friends and her friends' children in the parking lot, waiting for the cars parked in front of them to move along. This is where she introduced me to other kids who were going to boarding schools, as she tried to prepare me for my path ahead. She knew what to do to get me into a good school, and I was admitted into an all-male boarding school called Unity Model Secondary School in Agbarho. The school was only a few miles away from my family, but I was terrified. It was an all-boys school, and boys had always been my tormentors. My family reassured me that going to a boarding school was an opportunity for me to learn how to care for myself. Maybe I would even make some friends, they suggested.

The school was a large compound closed off by two gates. Palm trees exactly six feet apart lined the mile-long roundabout in front of the principal's office. When I arrived, we were told that for the first time ever, the school was also admitting girls. I was terrified to leave the comfort of my aunt's home, but she reminded me that she went to a boarding school in a nearby town where she learned all of the life skills that helped her build a life and career. Didn't I want that too? She gave me some pocket money and promised more would come each month. She left, driving through the roundabout as I stood with the matron, waving.

The matron asked me to take my bag and follow a senior student who was assigned to give me a tour of my room. He walked me around and showed me my bunk bed, helped me set up my mosquito net, and gave me a key to my locker. I was given a pair of bedsheets and a pillowcase, then was left alone to arrange my stuff. I could not do anything; I was already homesick, for my family and my privacy. The other boys were playing around, excited to be free.

In the evening, a boy ran to the bell under the tree in the middle of the compound and rang it to announce dinner. I got up slowly to go to the bathroom. Inside, naked boys were spraying water at each other. I washed my face, changed into the evening uniform, and then picked up my cutlery from my cupboard before heading to the dining hall. I spoke to no one, which felt like the safest approach.

We had a class schedule pasted in our hostel, five days of classes, Monday to Friday. On the weekend we had sanitation on Saturday morning, playtime in the afternoon, reading time in the evening. Sundays had church service in the morning, movies in the afternoon, and reading time in the evening. Everything was meticulously scheduled, and our only free time would be for an hour between nine and ten each night, before lights out.

Things began to warm up as I made some friends in my dorm. And soon I would find myself having my first sexual experience with another boy. It was in our dorm room, with thirty other bunk beds, each covered by mosquito netting. We had one cubic room, where the room master resided. Usually, a senior student was appointed to monitor junior students. One night during lights out, my classmate Eric crawled into my bed. He tried to play with me, asking me if I had ever done *this* before. I said no. It was an exciting new experience for me; even though I wanted to continue playing with him, I was too afraid we might get caught, so I asked him to leave.

Nothing happened further, but I continued to think of that experience and promised myself not to let anyone know I was interested in exploring more with Eric. Allowing or exploring those feelings would be admitting I was gay, and my strict Christian upbringing had made it clear liking another man was a sin worthy of condemnation to hell. I wanted to explore the feelings I had when he came under my mosquito netting, but the fear of retribution from my friends and family—or God—was too damning.

Slowly, though, I allowed myself to feel. When I returned to my aunt's home for the holiday, I had started developing feelings toward other guys that extended beyond lust. If my aunt found out, I knew, abstractly, that I would be in trouble—that my future opportunities would be jeopardized. My aunt, a reverent Christian living in Udu at this time, never missed church on Sunday. She got up early to dress me before driving half an hour to St. Andrew's Cathedral in Warri for a quick service. She grew up attending the cathedral and had made it an integral part of her life. Though living with my aunt was a strict and disciplined life, we had fun, too. Mrs. Erhimona's job provided her health care, a pension, and other benefits—such as an invitation to the company's holiday party for children at the end of each year. With me under her care, she could finally attend. We arrived at the center early. There was a bouncing castle with Barney and Mickey Mouse, and a dance competition for the kids that I gamely joined. My aunt said she was proud of me; even if it was my first time joining the kids, I wasn't shy—I jumped right onto the dance floor.

After the holidays, I returned to school. In my dormitory packed with young men, and despite my rigorous religious schedule with Mrs. Erhimona, I returned to the temptation of Eric.

I was about thirteen or fourteen years old when we started a budding friendship on the cusp of something deeper. Since our first encounter in my bed, we had become better friends. I warmed at the sound of his laughter. He was respected as a good soccer player, and he always stood up for me when other boys teased me. He was nice—he felt safe.

One night, when he crawled into my bed again, I thought it was a signal—that we shared a similar, private, and sinister desire. But it was a setup—Eric and my dorm mates had conspired to blackmail me, to prove I was gay, and they threatened to tell the school's administrators that I liked sleeping with other men. If everyone found out I was gay, I would be completely excommunicated, not only from my peers at the school but also from my church. My aunt, her church friends, and their children had all become my friends outside of school, and if they found out, I would lose them all. To keep them quiet, I started paying Eric and the others off, handing them some portion of my provisions, pocket money, and anything else that would ensure their discretion.

Even if as a teen I didn't fully understand my sexuality yet, I fully understood the backlash that would result in people finding out about my questioning of it. I remember in my mother's Pentecostal church, her pastor, an acclaimed prophet with foresight, once performed an exorcism of an evil spirit. I had seen what it was like to go through this experience—a ceremony performed in front of the entire congregation one Sunday morning, which involved the family gathering raw eggs, ants, salt, sugar, and baby chickens. These items were used to cleanse the bad spirit from its host, transmitting it to the animal for slaughter. This ceremony was burned in my mind—what would happen if this fate befell me?

I would find out eventually. After two years of extortion, my classmates reported me to the school's administration. The school suspended me and asked Mrs. Erhimona to come pick me up. There was only one solution—to pray the gay away. I would have to change my sexual orientation, by way of starving the demon within me by fasting, praying, and forcing myself to sleep with women. I was too young to sleep with a woman, but I was introduced to a wife-to-be—Esther—whom I would wed when I was old enough to marry. Other tactics were more extreme. People suggested severe punishment such as being tied with ropes and flogged to drive the demon out—a direct link to the Bible: Jesus had done the same to cast the demons from the two men in Matthew. My aunt would not subject me to such harsh treatment; she only wanted me to concentrate in school and wasn't concerned if I liked boys. She felt it was a phase and I would outgrow it.

After that, I lived with Mrs. Erhimona for almost four years. My experience living with her was fun, filled with laughs and an overarching sensibility of religious righteousness that she instilled in me. I was young and impressionable—her teachings left a mark on me, and in guiding myself on a path forward, which is perhaps what my parents wanted me to gain by living under her care.

Near the end of the fourth year, her husband asked me to return to my parents because he feared my influence on his son would be bad. I knew he worried not only about my reputation, but also the chance that I'd fall for his son. This was the beginning of a new reality: I was no longer a novice to the stigma of being suspected a homosexual. My life would be colored by ignorant narratives of pedophilia and acting like a woman. If only he knew how I hated the idea of going back to Warri to live with my parents. But I had no option. My aunt had to save her own relationship, and interfering or refusing her husband's instruction would mean the end of her marriage.

As I packed, Mrs. Erhimona entered with a warm smile.

"Do not worry, Edafe," she told me. "I will still pay your tuition. I will still care for you," she reassured me. She did not want to see me leaving her place, so she went into her room and locked herself inside. In my room, I cried as I packed.

Shortly after I left, Mrs. Erhimona became pregnant. She had never been pregnant until her late forties, which seemed an impossible feat. My family believes to this day that she was blessed by an angel of God just like Sarah, the wife of Abraham in the Bible, who got pregnant after menopause. The logic was that my aunt was a good woman, and God's blessing followed her goodness: if you do good things, good things would follow you; if you do bad things, you would be punished. I remember this as the overarching fear in my ability to confront the feelings stirring within me at this age.

When I returned to my family, my parents were in the early stage of their separation. My father had grown suspicious over the late hours my mother would keep ever since her beer parlor business had taken off years ago, believing that she was having affairs. My dad was angry at her—and angry about my return. He blamed my mother for the dysfunction in our family. It wasn't long until my father had a second wife of his own—which was far from unusual—and two other children. Banishing my mother from the home would be an easy way to move his second wife in.

Their dysfunction led me to a new plan—I asked my mother if I could go live with her sister, Mrs. Oyubu, and my grandmother, Mrs. Alice. Mrs. Oyubu had a son my age, my cousin Israel, and my mum agreed he could be a positive influence on me.

At age sixteen, I moved in with Mrs. Oyubu and began looking for guidance from another branch of my family. Mrs. Oyubu lived in Agbarho, where my boarding school was located, with her husband, her children, and stepchildren. My grandmother, Mrs. Alice, was a new addition to the pack since my days in Agbarho. Mrs. Alice was a fervent Christian just like Mrs. Erhimona. There was no way for me to escape going to church when living with my grandmother. None of Mrs. Oyubu's children liked going to church, but I had no option.

My grandmother would take me to her Pentecostal church on Sundays, whether I wanted to or not, even though Mrs. Oyubu's children did not attend. I would dress in slacks, a long-sleeve shirt, tie, and sneakers, all oversized. Arriving thirty minutes before the service began was late for Mrs. Alice. She arrived early, not to lift chairs or clean the hall for the service, but instead to chat with her friends. She took me to the adult section of the church, not the children's section, so she could show me off to her friends. I was a good boy, she would say, and I would be a shining light to her daughter's family. The church was the only place we could come together as a community; it was my amusement park as a young man. Christ, Mrs. Alice always told me, was the only hope I had of a good future.

I vividly remember the Sunday I arrived late—Mrs. Alice had left without me, because I did not get dressed on time. When I got to the church, the sermon had already begun. Worshippers sang in harmony, and the Holy Spirit was present in the room—one could tell of its presence when church members began speaking in tongues, as they were on that Sunday. I walked in wearing plain slacks, striped long-sleeve shirt well tucked in, and my shining brown shoes. My entrance distracted the roving spirit, and when the services ended Mrs. Alice was furious about my late arrival, opting to not speak to me as punishment. This feeling left a mark. If I wanted her care and affection, I would have to be a proper, upright Christian.

Faith became central to my life. Mrs. Alice made sure I understood that I would only be successful if I remained steadfast, attended service on time, prayed, and fasted. She decided to make it her duty to ensure I was never late again. And I wasn't—I became a rising star among the church's youth, in the eyes of the priests, ministers, and church elders. They all knew Edafe was Mrs. Alice's grandson. She even professed to some of her friends that her grandson would become a minister one day.

After Mrs. Erhimona's husband banished me for suspecting I was gay, I was left feeling an overwhelming sense of responsibility to make my family—my grandmother—happy with who I was. This was an opportunity for redemption. I knew then that I did not want to be gay; it was clear you could not be gay and a Christian. I was willing to do anything to combat the idea that I was a homosexual. Throughout my teenage years, I continually fought my urges. The most drastic way I sought absolution was to become a minister of the church. It was my belief that if I became a minister, God would deliver me from any evil spirit that had possessed me with my attraction for other men.

At eighteen, I was in college when I got ordained as a minister of the evangelical church, the Redeemed Christian Church of God student chapter in Enugu, Nigeria. Sunday mornings began with waking up as early as five in the morning to shower, get dressed, and join the prayer group at seven. I would arrive early to clean the halls with the women and welcome the prayer group at the church's gate, a Bible tucked under my arm. I greeted my brethren as they walked in, with a big handshake for the men and a broad-smiled nod for the women.

The services usually lasted for two and a half hours, but I'd spend my entire Sundays in the house of the Lord, and attended meetings, Bible studies, and prayer groups all week. Any breaks I had were spent reading the Bible and preparing for Sunday sermons.

I hoped—prayed—that the more time I devoted to my work as a minister, the better chances I'd have at ridding myself of my homosexual desires.

I was a student pastor, and outside of ministering in the church on Sundays, I tried to walk a straight path. In the Redeemed Christian Church of God, all ministers are encouraged to have a full-time job during the week or pursue an education at the same time and minister on weekends. In college, I dated a woman named Ese. We had an unspoken agreement. She wanted to flaunt a handsome boy to her friends without actually having sex; I wanted my friends to see me with a girlfriend, though I never treated her like one behind closed doors. When we broke up two years later, I needed a new shield. And what better disguise than becoming a pastor to ward off any questions about a girlfriend? A pastor could not have a girlfriend, as this was deemed fornication before marriage, and students could not be married.

Despite the many masks I wore, I saw them for what they were. I was a minister who professed something outwardly that I did not believe inwardly. I prayed, fasted—I would go days without eating solid food, only drinking water—and yet! I could not deny that I was still attracted to men.

Though the church was supposed to change me, it just created more shields. Being unable to date or marry women as a member of the church, I found myself constantly around men. The church allowed me not to be questioned by my friends in college, and my neighbors were not suspicious due to my mostly hooking up with straight-passing men who carried big Bibles under their arms too. We would meet, have sex, and in the morning, I would pray for forgiveness. Once, after having sex with another man, we prayed together for forgiveness. I believed my relationship with God was solid, but men would make you believe otherwise. The head pastors at my church always spoke of the destruction of people who acted like Sodom and Gomorrah in the Bible. Anti-gay messages were constant. While my head pastor spoke generally, I began to think he was speaking directly to me. I knew I didn't belong in the church, but I tried because the church had always been an integral part of my life. Being pushed away felt like being excommunicated from my own family. While I was fearful of destruction, I could not change who I was. To the church, I was steadfast, fervent, and diligent in prayers, but behind closed doors I continued to explore. Leading as a minister is a profound obligation. It began for me as a mask, but it grew into a burden that bled into every facet of my life. I had to be seen as upright; but being *seen* as upright didn't mean always having to *be* upright. To explore my sexuality would also mean protecting my public persona more vigilantly than before.

Eventually, the message about gay people made me very worried, so I decided to take a break from my role as a minister in the church at age twenty and focus on completing my education. I thought I could still practice my faith in God without being a pastor. But my time away from the church was clarifying. It helped me see that LGBTQ people are constantly told church is not a place for us. Our sins were inherent. The *us versus them* mentality could not have been clearer—we were made to feel like we did not deserve to exist.

I successfully hid my sexuality for a long time, until I tried to meet a guy on a gay dating website called Manjam. As we exchanged messages, he asked me about my sexual position preferences. I did not know, I told him truthfully—I hadn't had enough sexual experiences with men to really know what I liked. He asked me for nudes, which I took from the neck down. I did not bother to ask him for a photo in return, but we agreed to meet at his place in Enugu; there was no way he could come to the student lodge, a compound with seven rooms. Imagine the headline: STUDENT PASTOR CAUGHT HAVING SEX WITH ANOTHER MAN.

I took a cab to his place from the bus station in Enugu. He was waiting for me on the curb. He was not tall, but very muscular, which excited me. This was all so new, and I couldn't believe my luck: a hot man desired me. I found myself thinking ahead—that I might have a steady partner to visit regularly in Enugu.

He lived in a kind of slum with clustered houses, but he seemed warm and enthusiastic as we hit on each other walking to his apartment. When I finally got inside, he slammed the door shut. That was when three other guys jumped out of his closet.

They demanded my wallet and my phone, which I handed over, fearing for my life. A few of them went to an ATM to withdraw money from my account, while one held me hostage. He beat me with a belt until he got the call that they'd withdrawn money from my account. He asked me, "Why do you sleep with men when there are so many women?" I began to answer, to explain, only to be met with a punch. I lay with my face down as he continued to flog me with his belt. I tried to be strong at the beginning, but the belt started to cut through my skin, and I began sobbing. He would raise his belt and shout, "Keep quiet, you faggot!" as he continued to lash his belt against my back. I could not bear it, and I pleaded for him to stop, fearing that he would kill me. He shushed me, but I couldn't bear the pain any longer. The last time his belt left my back, I took the liberty and turned with my stomach facing up. "Please, please," I begged him. When the others returned with my card, they stripped me naked, threw my wallet and phone at me, and ordered me to run out and not look back.

I begged for my clothes, but all they gave me was my shorts. Outside, I had to ask strangers for money to return to school, all to no avail. I called my mother and lied to her, saying that I had been mugged. In Nigeria, people sell phone lines on the streets at umbrella-covered vendor stands. I made my way to one, where my mother sent me a phone card to sell, to pay for my transport back to school that evening.

I later learned that I had been what is called "kitoed," a scam common within the gay community in Nigeria. People log in to gay dating apps and pretend to be gay only to connect with people and ambush them. I found it nearly impossible to return to class after this. I spent three days in my room, trying to nurse my wounds and prevent my lodge mates from noticing my injuries. That would only lead to questions if my classmates and college knew I tried to meet a guy and had been beaten. They would only cheer on my attackers. I couldn't afford to lose the close connections I had with the boys in my class and compound. If I wanted to act on my desires, I'd have to be even more discreet.

I decided to look for someone to have sex with far away from my school in Enugu. There was a new social media app called 2Go that had chat groups for men. It was there that I met a DL (down-low) guy who lived in Anambra State, not too far from me—but just far enough to be neutral ground where I could feel safer to explore without being found out. Plus, he was older, in his fifties—I had always liked older people, probably from spending so much time with my aunts and Mrs. Alice. He was brief with every sentence, which made me worried he was just another person looking to blackmail me. I tried to get him to reveal himself—what sort of sexual positions did he prefer, for example? He would laugh it off and told me I would find out if we met. Perhaps this should have been a red flag, but laughing off my questions only made him more intriguing. We exchanged information, and eventually he invited me to Anambra. I prepared a bag and headed there for a weekend journey. I was of course naïve to make this journey, but the man sounded mature and obscure—and discreet.

After a short drive from Agbani in Enugu State, where my college is located, to Onitsha, a popular town in Anambra, a neighboring state to Enugu, I met him in Onitsha market, a popular open-air market filled with women who sold goods and food in the shade. I was happy to meet him in a public place after my last encounter. He called me before I could find him, and he asked what I was wearing.

"A navy-blue shirt," I said, "and a face cap." Soon, he drove closer to me in a dark car and rolled down the passenger-side window.

"Come in," he said.

When I got inside, he immediately apologized for making me wait. "I just wanted to play it safe—wow," he said. "You're young."

I laughed. "The feeling is mutual. You look like my father." We both laughed, and I felt a weight lift. He was very inquisitive, asking about my family, and my friends in college, if they knew I liked men. If I was open about my sexuality.

"Actually," I said, "I was a pastor for the last few years."

Finally, he asked, "So, how long have you been doing this?"

I thought about how honest to be. But he hadn't given me a reason to lie.

"Frankly, I'm new to this. I have tried to meet people before, but they blackmailed me." I turned to him. "What about you?"

He did not respond, just kept on smiling and rolling his tongue as if to say something, but he did not say anything further.

The path to his house was all rural farmlands, a beautiful sight covered in red sand. We got to the gate of his building, a gigantic structure with a crucifix at the top. Inside, there was a giant bell in the middle of the compound, and just beyond that he parked his car under a tree.

"You are my fellow priest friend, younger brother," he said, turning to me. "I told my colleagues that my friend from the seminary is going to school and that he asked me to give him some money."

"You're a reverend father?" I asked. He did not answer my question, but he didn't need to.

He only asked me if I understood, but he never asked if I was comfortable, or explained to me before I packed my bag in Agbani what I was going into, and now he did not care if I was uneasy with the plan. I guessed this wasn't his first time doing this.

He walked out of the car, expecting me to follow him, but I found myself paralyzed in the passenger seat, watching him greet people on the lawn who had arrived for prayer. Suddenly, I did not want to continue this exploration. I thought about leaving when someone approached the car and asked if they could carry my luggage inside. I clung to my bag.

"Are you okay?" she asked.

"Leave my bag alone, I am fine," I replied, not smiling.

"Hey!" she yelled over to the man. "Is this your priest friend?"

"Yes," he yelled back. I was still uneasy, but I followed them back toward the vestry, a small house at the side of the church. His apartment was on the top floor, and he guided me inside.

"Please be comfortable," he insisted kindly. "And do not leave the room for any reason. I am joining the other priests for evening prayers." He smiled and left. I had heard stories of people in the eastern part of Nigeria using gay men for sacrificial rituals, to make *blood money*, as they call it. At the same time, I had to remind myself: He is a priest. I am in a church. I am safe.

While he was away, my food was brought in, and I had dinner while sitting down on his bed. I tried to sleep but couldn't. I didn't want to have sex with a priest, and I hoped he would understand that. Though I had become a priest to hide my sexuality—and had indeed had sex with men as a priest myself—I could think of no greater sin than having sex with another priest.

I heard the doorknob turn and the hair stood up on my hands.

He smiled as he entered. "Would you like a drink?"

"No," I said.

He poured himself a drink and sat down.

"I know you are afraid; I am sorry I did not tell you I'm a priest."

"That's a lot of information not to tell me, don't you think?"

"I'm often afraid," he said, "of being caught. Being attacked. Surely you can understand? If you're not comfortable, we don't have to do anything. I'm okay with that."

"Yes," I said. "I don't want to sleep with a priest, I can sleep on the floor."

He refused to let me sleep on the floor. I agreed to sleep on the bed, but only if he promised not to try to touch me. That night, he crawled on top of me. I balled my fist tightly, tensed my body. He could tell I was awake, that I was refusing, and still he begged.

"I haven't done this in a while," he said. "I would be glad if you'd agree to play with me. I will give you more than the cost of your transportation when you leave tomorrow."

I continued shaking my head. "No, no, no!" But he persisted.

We cussed and fussed around the bed until the late hours of the evening before he finally gave up and went to sleep. He had an early morning mass to deliver, after all.

The sun could not rise fast enough, and I was already awake when it peeked over the horizon and found that the priest had already left.

My views about sex have become more liberal since that evening, but back then, I felt the rules and regulations of the church weighing heavily upon me. A priest was meant to be a standard of uprightness and goodness. Seeing a priest act this way shattered me. But he was also a person with wants and desires, just like me.

I got up to shower and pack my bag. But I would need to go find him in the church—I couldn't get home without the money he promised for my transportation. When I walked inside, mass had started, and he was standing at the altar with another minister, giving out communion.

I sat at the back of the church, wondering if this moment would feel different if we had had sex.

A church member approached me with an envelope—inside was the money for my return trip. We did not exchange parting words, and I never saw him again. But I thought of him often in the days and years to come. I returned to my college in Enugu State with a new perspective on religion and its suppression. Here was this fifty-year-old man living in the shadows, hiding who he was. Using his priest status to mingle and guide younger men, hiding his sexuality behind a cloak of religion. Did I want that for myself, decades from now? Worse yet, what if I had not been so lucky?

I found myself ready for a new form of freedom. Still, I was struggling to be somebody I wasn't—I wanted to be upright and righteous, yet popular and accepted, also with a desire to be free of the burden I carried, which is living in fear of rejection, afraid to come out, and the potential backlash from my family. Opening up would be a reminder that I don't fit in on the path I was expected to follow. And the pain of living this lie and the resistance I was facing from being honest caused me suffering.

Shortly after this, I heard that my grandmother, Mrs. Alice, was very ill, and she had been brought to my mum's place to live out her final days, so I returned to Warri to see her and my family. My grandmother was living in the compound given to my mother as part of my grandfather's inheritance after he passed away. The building was a big compound that housed multiple rooms and had three storefronts attached. Separate from the main building and attached to the stores was a boys' quarter. My grandmother was in one of the small rooms at the quarters, where she had been moved to for her final days.

My mother was sitting with Mrs. Alice on the bed when I entered. When she left for the kitchen, I looked at Mrs. Alice, who had grown so frail it seemed death was near. It dawned on me that I didn't want her to die not knowing who I was.

I took her hand. "Grandmother," I began, my voice a bit shaky. The room was empty and silent but for our shared breathing. "I need you to know before you go that I am gay."

She turned and hugged me. "I love you, my grandson," she said. It was simple, but it was all I needed to hear. I felt a lightness.

After coming out to my grandmother in Warri and returning to my college in Enugu, I knew I had to leave Enugu State—my experiences there had made me grow to despise it. I needed to be somewhere safer, and Warri was not an option; my dad had blamed my mum when they learned of my indiscretion at school, and my mum had begun to second-guess her undying support for me. I had to find people like me, a community where I could openly be myself. Telling my grandmother was not the same as being open to the community in Warri. The only gay friends I had at this time were folks I'd met in Facebook groups, who all lived in large cities. In Nigeria, the only place gay people could live openly in relative safety was in bigger cities like Lagos or Abuja, which meant after I graduated, I was left with two options: to move to Abuja or Lagos City. I had taken to message boards online and began chatting with folks in Abuja—I was told there were safe houses there for gay people who had left their families. Some of the people in these groups were even ex-priests, too.

Arriving in Abuja was like setting foot on a new planet. The roads were wide, the buildings big; it carried an ambience, an energy, of places I'd only seen in movies. Still, I had no family there, knew no one, and only had an address given to me by someone in the message boards. I was told that the owner of the house, Bobby, accepted gay people from around the country who were eager to learn a trade and start fresh. Bobby was a well-connected member of the community; no matter who I asked online, people spoke highly of him, of his courage. What struck me most was that he was openly gay—he had been kitoed in the past but was seemingly no longer ashamed or afraid of anything. I was told that gay men who lived with Bobby had some class (they are the Abuja gays that dress expensively and take cabs instead of public transport). They had found opportunities for success in Abuja, and Bobby was their queen mother. He provided a safe haven for the many gay people who fled to Abuja each year, searching for a life of their own. I was no different. I just hoped Bobby would take me under his wing.

Bobby's house was along the Abuja expressway, a compound made up of two buildings, a parking space for two cars, a doghouse, and a generator that hummed outside. As I approached his gate, a neighbor told me that Bobby wasn't back from work yet. Was I that obvious in my pursuit of him? I grew worried about what it meant that people could so easily mark me, a wayward gay man looking for the queen mother. I held my backpack tightly, sat on a row of stones in front of the compound, and watched people walk on the pathway along the expressway. In the north, people dressed differently than those in Warri—they wore Arab attire, women in hijabs, men in caftans and round hats. I remember being amazed by the horticulture around Bobby's house, which was nothing like what I had seen in Warri or Enugu. Flowers were planted along the curbside, and the grass on the side of the road was stylized to read "Welcome to Abuja." Most impressive to me was that there was so much space in between the houses.

After some time, four men drove up to the gate in a white Toyota Camry and honked. I moved aside so the car could drive into the compound. A tall, heavyset man with dreadlocks got out of the car and walked toward me.

"What are you doing in my front yard?" he asked.

"I came to see Bobby," I said.

"Do you know who Bobby is?"

"I don't." I explained I was given this address and told to tell Bobby I'd just arrived in Abuja looking for a place to stay.

The large man scanned me with his big bulging eyes and said, "Come inside."

That was how I met Bobby and his entourage.

In Bobby's place the boys were freer to be themselves, at least for a while. People chose new names, he explained. Under his care, you would learn a trade—usually hairstyling, like Bobby—and graduate from Bobby's home onto starting your own business and renting your own apartment. The boys in Bobby's place came from all over the country—they did not all speak the same language, but they all shared an ambition to be something they were not before arriving in Abuja. A few of them had completed high school, but none of them went to college—most were chased out of their family homes at a young age or fled from the suffocation. I felt lucky to have completed my bachelor's degree, majoring in food science and technology at Enugu State University, before I arrived to Abuja. But I saw in them something I never saw before, the desire to be who you *wanted* to be. There was an openness to them, sharing their stories, inviting me to eat without contributing, showing me new clothes and customs. I felt comfortable. I felt at home.

I had a degree in food science and did not want to become a hairstylist. I came to Abuja to look for an opportunity to start a new life; maybe I had planned to make some money, learn more about the world, and then return home to start a family in Warri. That idea quickly evaporated.

The weekend I arrived at Bobby's I was quickly initiated into the Abuja way of doing things, which meant I was going to become a gay man with taste. There was a level of sophistication Abuja gay men possessed that was far from anything I was used to in my hometown in Warri. They were visible compared to my experience in Enugu or elsewhere in the southeastern part of Nigeria. They took care of one another in the community, embraced their differences as society framed them to be weirdos. I had the opportunity to attend my first underground gay party, the locations of which were only shared an hour before the event's start. You'd arrive well-dressed, but as soon as you went underground, out came the gowns, wigs, and high heels. This first party was held in a rich man's bungalow in the middle of nowhere. A space was cleared for dancing, men ambling about, drinking and chatting, as drag queens started to emerge.

I remember my jaw dropping.

The queens were so pretty—but also, so bold, so brave. To do this in Nigeria! They wore amazing outfits, Zac Posen–esque dinner gowns, elegantly tight on the waist and free at the bottom.

I turned to Bobby in amazement. "Come on, darling." He laughed. "You are in Abuja. This is not your village in Warri." The music kicked the party into a different gear, with disco lights and a very funny MC dragging the queens' names: Michael became Michelina, Austin became Augusta. The party went on for hours, with drag queens competing for prizes. People walked around having conversations with new guests like me. I would meet many of my closest new friends at these functions, people like Emmanuel, a bulky gay man in his late thirties who moved to Abuja when he became HIV positive in order to find a community for support. Like me, he arrived with nothing, having left behind his family in Benin at the age of seventeen without finishing high school. When we met, he was working as a tailor while also getting his master's and his apprenticeship. He hoped to have a shop of his own and employ his own apprentice who he could teach and mentor. We met on the ballroom dance floor and instantly clicked—he had a natural empathetic air and was very down-to-earth and approachable. When Bobby was not available to attend balls, Emmanuel and I would go together.

Through both him and Bobby, I learned these balls weren't only for fun and festivities—people were encouraging guests to get tested for HIV, too. They were fun; but they were also educational, resources for the community I was being adopted into. These gatherings served us in not only building community but also keeping it safe.

I felt seen; I felt welcomed. Perhaps for the first time in my life. I knew immediately that night that there was no way I could return to Warri. Abuja was the place for me.

I began to learn more about Bobby, too. He was out to his family, and at thirty-nine, he had never married a woman. His family did not disturb him, and he had made his point clear: accept me for who I am, or you have no place in my life. He once had a hair salon in Lagos but had to leave after too many people learned of his sexuality. Prior to moving to Lagos, Bobby had a salon in Enugu. He was attacked in his salon for attempting to go on a date with someone masquerading as gay. He had had an opportunity to go out with a gay man who seemed interested in him. The guy recorded the conversation he had with Bobby. Unfortunately, Bobby believed he was genuinely interested in guys and spoke with him like he would with someone within the gay community. A day after the date, the guy had spread the recording to other homophobic people who then came to raid Bobby's hair salon—not dissimilar to what happened to me at university.

Bobby came to Abuja to have a fresh start, which is why he maintained a hard line with people who stayed with him. He had a golden rule: while you lived with him, you did not sleep with him. You worked in Bobby's salon and followed his rules, until he felt you'd earned your independence. My case was different, though. Perhaps because I was not working in his salon—because I had a college degree and could look for a professional job—or for other reasons, sometimes he let me stay in his room. He was a big man. I like men who are thick in the right places, and Bobby held me tight; I always felt safe in his arms. He was the first person I had sex with when I moved to Abuja as an out gay person to myself and the community, and it was a revelation: no one chased me in the street, no one exposed me as a priest. For once, there were no consequences. I found myself lusting after him and this new sense of security. I wanted to be around Bobby all the time.

But nobody shared Bobby's heart—or bed—for long. He frequently brought in lovers from out of state, and on those nights, I slept on the couch. I was new to being gay, I thought it was going to be me and Bobby only, but in Nigeria you meet different people for self-preservation. You didn't want to be seen with the same man all the time, and you didn't want to mistakenly show too much public affection. As I learned more of the rules, I thought more about why I had come. It was to be free, but also to build a life. I couldn't rely on Bobby to take care of me all the time. I would need to find a job, save money, and build something for myself.

It took time, but I gradually found my footing. After a few months I got a job in Abuja as a program officer for Family Health International working on a USAID-funded project called SIDHAS: Strengthening Integrated Delivery of HIV/AIDS Services. I found a room to rent, through the grapevine of the gay community. I moved out of Bobby's place and into an apartment of my own, which I shared with two other gay men in Abuja. Though I had roommates, I was really living on my own for the first time—no mama, no Bobby, no one to turn to when I found myself in trouble. Emmanuel began to visit more often—he taught me how to cook or would take me to a ball to lose myself in a crowd of people. He was a free-spirited person and never wanted me to sit in my room alone, wallowing in self-pity for pursuing my dreams.

Eventually, I wanted to pursue a master's degree and was accepted to study nutrition at Ahmadu Bello University Zaria in Kaduna State, which was about two hundred miles from Abuja. I was struggling financially—on top of room and board for school, tuition, and rent, I needed help. So, I called home. Mrs. Erhimona offered to pay my tuition, and my mum and elder sister Ovoke, who had returned from Ghana and was now living in Warri with her husband, helped me pay my rent. I felt conflicted, relying on my family for money while at the same time keeping my distance from them—they knew that I had moved north to avoid their constant harassment to get married. As much as I felt out of place with them—my new life rubbing up against my old one—I missed them. But I was learning how to cultivate a new family. I had my roommates. I had Bobby and Emmanuel.

I was proud of the life I was building, but it took hard work. I was very busy taking care of myself and working toward my degree. I found myself having less time for attending balls. But about three months into living on my own, my phone rang. It was Bobby's older sister. Bobby had collapsed at the salon and died.

My entire world became smaller. No one was certain of the cause of death. The rumors were that he had died from HIV complications; others said he was poisoned, due to his open-door policy. I was devastated. By the time I returned to Abuja, Bobby had been buried. His funeral had brought so many members of his beloved community in Abuja together. Friends and family gathered at his place afterward. Many cried, sharing laughs and good memories of Bobby, this larger-than-life person who had somehow helped all of us. His circle knew we were close, which also put me in danger because the closeness and disclosure to his family—who were dealing with the grief of their son, brother, uncle, and cousin—would further stir up their emotions and be a reminder that folks like me contributed to why Bobby never got married or had kids. The community was already facing increased attacks due to the passage of a new law, the Same-Sex Marriage (Prohibition) Act, popularly known as SSMPA, signed by the Nigerian president in January 2014. The new law criminalized same-sex relationships, punishing the guilty with up to fourteen years in prison. For men like me in Nigeria, life was changing. Our thriving community was quickly driven back underground.

Bobby's death sent shock waves through the gay community in Abuja. If he was poisoned, could that happen to us too, if we lived out in the open like Bobby did? With the passage of SSMPA, the police began to crack down harder on the underground gay community. Not only did the law criminalize same-sex relationships, but it also criminalized activism and groups supporting gay rights. But perhaps the most devastating effects of this law was the fear—men who have sex with men (MSM) became afraid to approach health care providers for treatment and prevention resources. HIV infections among gay men soared. One could draw a correlation between this and the increasing rate of HIV infections among MSM in the general population—at the time, MSM had an infection rate of 29.9 percent, as opposed to about 3–4 percent* in the general population.

* George I.E. Eluwa et al., "Rising HIV prevalence among men who have sex with men in Nigeria: a trend analysis," *BMC Public Health* 19, no. 1201 (2019), https://bmcpublichealth.biomedcentral.com/articles/10.1186/s12889-019-7540-4.

Gay people would not have spaces to exist anymore, and both citizens and the police made sure of it. The police began to receive tips from citizens about suspected gay community members or addresses where gay parties were supposed to be held. I worried not only for my safety—but also for my family. How would they react were they to learn I had been imprisoned, or worse, killed, for being gay? Some discrimination extended beyond taunts and public humiliation—it was outright violent. Gay men soon became the targets of vigilantes, as mob violence increased. The underground parties stopped—any gathering of men was an opportunity for police to antagonize. In seven Muslim states that practice sharia law in Nigeria, being gay could be punishable with death by stoning.

The worst incident I can recall was in January 2014, when the Abuja police force was alerted to the planned massacre of gay men in Gishiri, a popular gay slum comprised of about eight rooms housing nearly thirty people with nowhere to go. When SSMPA passed, non–state actors began targeting communities like Gishiri because they were easy targets and had few protections. Angry mobs showed up with machetes, car tires, and petroleum, planning to capture and burn these men utilizing these items. When the police intervened, it wasn't to stop the mob; rather, they arrested the suspected gay men in Gishiri, and though the mob was unsuccessful, neither were they charged with any crimes.

This set a precedent—you could harm gay people and no charges would be brought against you. Even if the law was or wasn't enforced, it emboldened discrimination against gay men in everyday situations. I recall a report of a man who went to a pharmacy to get condoms and lubricants. He waited in a long line to pay, and when he got to the cashier, she said out loud, so everyone in the store could hear, "Why is he buying lubricants? Women do not need lubricants since they are lubricated already. Sir, are you gay?" They argued; she raised her voice; and quickly, other shoppers joined in his humiliation, taunting him, screaming slurs and obscenities until he fled the store . . . *Look at you, woman wrapper. You have the guts to insult a woman. We don't blame you, because you already look like a woman, Mtcheew! Look at his ass. Big ass, woman ass! You allow men to fuck you. Your parents should have not given birth to you. You waste! Ashawo! Gay! Gay! Gay!*

In February 2014 the police were tipped off to a suspected gay marriage. There were rumors of an underground gathering where men were getting married illegally—the police raided this gathering and arrested everyone in attendance. These two attacks resulted in gay people refusing to gather anymore; our community went deeper into hiding. In effect, we felt this was the purpose of SSMPA—to create so much stigma around gay people that we'd have no choice but to go into hiding, which of course erased our public existence in Nigeria, as well as having serious ramifications for our survival where access to health care services were concerned.

I was a novice when I arrived in Abuja, and Bobby inspired me. I remember feeling his mission was so noble—and that I, too, wanted to provide a space for people to feel welcome, especially those who had fled to the cities due to violence. But Bobby was gone—and slowly, more and more of my peers fell victim, either to policing or complications for lack of good health care.

Before Bobby's death, we had an urgent need for community and safety—after his death, even more so. Though I was terrified of retribution, I attended peer education seminars to watch and listen from the sidelines. I wanted to learn more about how I could help—and the conversations galvanized me. I joined more groups with missions set for equality and education. I saw so much misinformation being spread, particularly about HIV—many gay men in these groups believed HIV could only be transmitted through vaginal sex. It was clear that both the laws and a lack of information were perpetuating this health crisis within our community. So I joined an organization in Abuja that advocated for access to health care treatment for the MSM community.

Thinking back to my days on the debate team, it probably shouldn't have surprised me that my vocal nature made me a leader of a movement that I had initially wanted nothing to do with, for fear of my own safety. The fight for gay men's access to health care treatment became my life's work. Though many of my colleagues didn't even have college degrees, they had a wealth of knowledge—and a real desire to help, to teach people what they knew. It was often overwhelming—reliving the violence I'd seen in my university days, alongside losing my closest allies—and at first I went into shock, but then I took action.

This was my first introduction to activism: conducting peer-to-peer education sessions; standing up for sick MSM when they found themselves in clinics; motivating people who tested positive for HIV to take the proper medications, as well as how to properly use condoms and lubricants to prevent the spread of HIV infections. Suddenly I was an educator who found a voice in a community that needed one.

It was around this time that Emmanuel became very ill due to his refusal to access treatment, and could not leave his house. I went to visit him and was immediately shocked. He had lost a lot of weight; he could barely talk; the scent of death wafted through his apartment.

I asked him if I could take him to see a doctor. When he hesitated, I asked him to explain why.

Emmanuel said, "The last time I went to the clinic, the nurse said I have anal warts because I have gay sex." I tried to explain that anal warts were a symptom of HPV, which is not a disease that only affected MSM. He needed treatment, and he could get it, but he was too ashamed from his experience last time to take the option seriously.

A few weeks later, he was dead, too. I hadn't been around for Bobby's death, but watching Emmanuel waste away was a wake-up call—and a call to action. Was I next?

I began working for a human rights organization in the summer of 2014, fighting for access to health care services for gay men. We organized peer-to-peer learning programs and established a support group for gay men living with HIV. Our activism, like most activism in gay Nigerian communities, was heavily rooted in HIV/AIDS work, sensitization, awareness, and prevention strategies. Our organization was designed as a health clinic, but we offered resources and information discreetly to those who needed it. Soon, our clinic's human rights desk became the hotline for our community. Until one day in March of 2016, the police showed up to raid our office. It was clear they were looking for evidence to incriminate us as gay men. They searched, but all they could find were dildos, condoms, lubricants, diagrams of penises, and sexual health education material. This alone wasn't enough to incriminate us legally. But it did highlight a new opportunity. Perhaps if we could educate law enforcement officers on human rights and the needs of the MSM community, we could create change. So I worked Mondays through Fridays at the clinic, even putting in time on the weekends, to formulate a plan of action.

We received a grant from NED, the National Endowment for Democracy, to help strengthen intergovernmental relations with democratic practice in Abuja. We are asked to provide human rights trainings to law enforcement officers. I educated law enforcement officials about the impact of the raids on stigmatization and how it increased HIV infections within our community. It was not an easy process. Most of the officers were not receptive to the information, but we knew we had to keep trying. The grant from the National Endowment for Democracy in Washington, D.C. helped position the training as a foreign relations program and not a local program. It was understood as an open democracy forum with meetings held on the weekends at the Sheraton Abuja Hotel. The officers had to attend in person and sign in on a roster to receive stipends. The stipends act as a motivating factor for the police officers to attend. I believe the free food and air-conditioning was what really brought them to the trainings, though. Some of the officers surprised me and were receptive to learning more—which helped me create a back channel with some sympathetic officers that I would need in the future, for bailing out friends from jail after police raids.

After a police raid, folks in our community were hesitant to help those who were jailed, for fear of more harassment or extortion, or for bringing suspicion upon themselves of being gay. Though the officers of whom I had made allies would help us do this safely, our community was still being targeted and driven underground. Working as an activist means knowing the law well enough to not have it used against you; working as a community organizer and peer educator was the only way I could stand up for other members in my community. I did this work for two years, 2014 to 2016, making new friends, teaching the ropes of the city to new arrivals, and working to bring our community out from the darkness. I felt firsthand the weight of being a leader within a marginalized community. I was a figurehead, a target of law enforcement and non–state actors. Vigilantes often prayed on me during my walks to and from work. Getting dressed in the mornings, I'd ask myself if I looked passing enough. Passing is dressing as a masculine man, which meant not deviating from gender norms. A heterosexual man would not have an ear piercing of any kind; they wear slack pants, not too short or tight, to get to work safely or visit the police station to pay someone's bail without being harassed as a gay person. Though I never set out to be an activist, I found it came to me quite naturally. In other ways, it was easy. The more people we lost, especially those closest to me like Bobby and Emmanuel, the more I felt driven to fight. It was clear I was walking into fire—but I would rather have been burned fighting for change than be burned slowly on the sidelines, watching members of my community die, while waiting for my turn. I had no way out. It seemed activism, in a sense, became a new guiding principle that took residence within me in the space religion had once held.

* * *

In early 2016, when I was living in the Durumi district of Abuja, I had two roommates—Sylvester and Sly—but they soon left for America to seek political asylum based on their sexual orientation. So I found myself living alone in a compound with no fence (what we call a "face-me-I-slap-you"), that was very open to passersby. Most of my neighbors were married with children; I stood in stark contrast, single and childless. They would jokingly probe, "Edafe, when are you going to marry?" I did not concern myself with these minor suspicions and went about doing my work, but the constant violence against gay men led to a paranoia. I was anxious and afraid that I would be next; perhaps it was due to living alone, but I felt the day my secrets would be exposed was on the horizon.

Early in the morning on my birthday, I was startled awake by a loud noise. "Edafe! Edafe!" voices suddenly chanted from outside. "Open the door! We know you are gay, and we are going to kill you!" Residents of Durumi had formed a mob, gathered outside my compound. I woke up feeling my heart pounding in my chest; I could not think or reasonably judge what was happening. I knew I needed to move quickly, but I was paralyzed. I thought I could hop out the back window, if they were at the front of my building. So, wearing just my underwear, I raced to the window, ready to jump. But the mob had surrounded my compound on all sides. Soon they broke down my door and dragged me into the streets. I was flogged with sticks, cutlasses, and anything they could find, beating me unconscious while children sang and cheered and clapped behind us. *Gay! Gay! Gay!*

When I woke up in the clinic, I was confused, and worried I would not recover from the attack. I was told a Good Samaritan had saved me, which was only a slight relief to the terrible pain I felt all over my body. *If there is a God, they just saved me*, I remember thinking. I wondered then if my family knew—about what happened to me, and about why it happened.

Though there were so many mysteries about the attack, I knew one thing for certain: I wouldn't be alive much longer if I stayed in Nigeria.

Before the attack, I had been invited to a conference in the United States, taking place in December—could this be my way out? I had always envisioned America to be a beacon of hope, having seen gay men live their lives openly in the States. I remembered my friend Kent, who worked for the U.S. government and regularly visited Nigeria—a gay man who was openly married to another man in Brooklyn, New York. He led me to believe life in America could be better for gay people. I wanted to apply for a visa, but the U.S. visa office would not allow you to apply for a visa until 120 days before the intended trip. So instead, I opted for the fastest visa I could obtain—within seventy-two hours, I found myself in the UAE, where I stayed for two weeks and figured out my escape plan.

I returned from the UAE in the middle of August, but I could no longer work for the human rights organization, as I needed to keep a lower profile. I spent time hiding with my friend Uche at his place on the outskirts of the city. For me to survive, I got a job as a consultant back at Family Health International in Abuja where I had started my journey.

Two months passed like a breeze, just pushing paper, making money to help pay Uche's rent and minding my business and my safety. One day in October of 2016, I was in my office, digging through a pile of paperwork, when my phone buzzed. It was a text from Uche.

Edafe Where are you?

I am in the office, I replied.

You have to leave now!

This message followed with a link to an article. Apparently, I was being given an award for my work as a grassroots advocate for the MSM community, by a foundation called AVAC in New York City. What should have been a proud moment quickly turned dark—due to the SSMPA, community members were encouraged to alert local authorities of known homosexuals. And the article was already online. I could be turned into the police, or worse yet, killed.

This single blazing moment brought my life in Nigeria to an end. I had to run—the farther, the better.

CHAPTER TWO

Becoming a Refugee and Claiming Asylum

In recent decades, the global population of refugees and asylum seekers has increased substantially. In 2019 alone, over 79.5 million people were forcibly displaced.* Of those 79.5 million displaced persons, 4.2 million were asylum seekers, and 1 in 113 people on earth is an asylum seeker, has been internationally displaced, or is a refugee. This has coincided with global nationalist trends that have led to greater scrutiny of, and hostility toward, immigrants, refugees, and asylum seekers. Many refugees flee in a hurry. Ours are often life or death situations, especially for LGBTQ refugees. In many countries, including Jamaica, Iran, and Sudan, LGBTQ individuals are persecuted, imprisoned, and sometimes sentenced to death based on their sexual orientation or gender identity. Many experience the same kind of public outing

* Filippo Grandi, UN High Commissioner for Refugees, UNHCR Flagship Reports, *UNHCR—Global Trends Forced Displacement in 2019* (released June 18, 2021), https://www.unhcr.org/flagship-reports/globaltrends/globaltrends2019/.

that I faced. Transgender individuals may be victims of forced sterilization or castration, so-called "corrective rape," domestic violence, forced sex work, institutionalized violence at the hands of the police, or death. We are often blackmailed; we often go into hiding until we can gather the funds to flee. I was lucky enough to have a U.S. visa and savings.

While this certainly happens in Africa—many other West Africans move to South or East Africa to work for some time, before traveling to South America—this is a global phenomenon. In 2017, an anti-gay "purge" took place in Chechnya, Russia, leaving LGBTQ Russians with twenty-four to seventy-two hours to leave their homes. A similar incident occurred in Brunei in 2019 after their government passed anti-gay legislation, leaving LGBTQ people with less than a month to flee before the law went into effect. Uganda's "Kill the Gays" bill led to LGBTQ people having to flee or face death. There is not a single way to flee, but we have a common destination: a safe place where we can find the freedom to express who we are.

As soon as my friend alerted me that my name had been published regarding the AVAC honor, I found myself running toward the highway, shouting and flailing my hands, to hail a cab.

When a cab finally stopped, the driver asked me where I was going. Though I was staying with Uche, I'd left my documents and all my belongings behind at my apartment where the mob had attacked me. I did not know if I would find any of my belongings, but I would not be able to leave Nigeria without my passport and some key documents I had gathered in hopes of restarting my life. We sped toward my place. A sensation of great astonishment dawned on me: my time here had come to an end.

Fearing someone would recognize me, I asked the driver to wait outside while I gathered my things. I drew a file from under my mattress of all my certificates: my diploma, birth certificate, the local government of origin card, and my baptism certificate. I could only take enough clothing to fit into my backpack. I stood up to breathe, and looked around one last time. So this was it. I found myself again leaving a place I'd called home.

I had the cab take me to Uche's place a few miles away, where I could stay for a few days before anyone suspected he was hiding me. There, I would get my plans in order while waiting for my paycheck to clear, and buy a plane ticket. I stayed with him for three days before moving to a hotel near the international airport in Abuja. I was paranoid, nervous, afraid—I found comfort in chain-smoking cigarettes and fixating on my escape. On the other side, life would be better—if I made it out of here alive.

None of my family knew where I was. I wanted to call them, especially my mother, to tell her I was leaving Nigeria, with no plans to return. But I couldn't risk my safety—or theirs. If I succeeded in escaping, my mother would be able to speak to me one day. I wasn't ready to give my life for my freedom. I wanted both.

The next morning, when my office called asking about my whereabouts, I told them I was sick. Apparently I needed to sign a time sheet before they could pay me, and we argued over the phone until the money arrived. The only flight I could afford was on Egypt Air leaving the next day for Cairo, with an overnight connection to New York City.

This would be my last night in Nigeria for a long time, I realized. I began to wonder what it would mean to leave everything behind. All I could do to escape myself, to stop worrying even for a few moments, was to drink and smoke. I stayed up until four in the morning, unable to sleep, and woke up groggy to my alarm a few hours later.

Boarding would begin in just an hour.

I washed my face, brushed my teeth, and skipped showering. In the airport, I found myself constantly glancing behind me, turning side to side, fearing still I might be recognized. Typical of a Nigerian airport were street hawkers at the terminal trying to sell you snacks and clothing to take abroad, but I had no interest. I waited at my gate, breathless, until I found myself aboard the plane moments later.

This should have been one of the happiest moments of my life—freedom, survival. But I was engulfed by sadness. I was giving up on the possibility of building a life in Nigeria. I was giving up my family. Though my friends knew my whereabouts, I was giving them up too. I might not return to Nigeria for a long time. Maybe never again.

And then, suddenly, I saw the green grass of the plains gradually fading into thick cloud cover. I had escaped, and the weight of this fact pressed down upon me. I closed my eyes; when I opened them, a flight attendant was tapping my shoulder to enthusiastically tell me *we are here!*

* * *

In Cairo, we had to leave our passports with the security at the airports to prevent people in transit from fleeing into Egypt. It is mandatory for passport control to keep all the passengers' passports with connecting flights from Cairo. Airlines had to ensure their passengers wouldn't escape, so with our passports stripped of us, we were taken by bus to a hotel in Cairo to spend the night. Though I had left my immediate threat behind in Nigeria, I was still rattled. What if the airline and passport control officers in Cairo discovered I was going to seek asylum and refused to let me board my connection? What if I overslept and missed my flight to New York? I had always dreamed of going to America, but not like this.

Sleep was brief. I awoke early, at five a.m., to meet the bus back to the airport, a massive building that surpassed most of my expectations of other African airports. Inside, I was constantly looking for danger when there was none. My heart raced, assuming people could tell I was gay—Egypt was not a safe place for LGBTQ people either, I reminded myself. As I approached the passport control desk, the agent looked me up and down. After a moment, she handed me my documents. "Everything is in order," she said. Soon, I was ascending into the clouds, and again I was in awe of how beautiful this place was that I was escaping; I sat close to the window, looking at the calmness of the Mediterranean Sea. *Finally.* I allowed myself a sigh of relief. I was on my last leg to freedom.

The trip from Cairo to New York was eleven hours. During the long flight, most passengers went into deep sleep. Some watched movies. A couple to my right reminisced aloud about their beautiful vacation to Africa. I, however, was in a full panic—sweating, unable to sleep. I was heading into a mysterious future in America. What would happen when I landed? No one in my family had ever been to America before, let alone lived there. The fear I harbored was not based on nothing. I did not have the courage to leave everything behind. I felt like a failure, abandoning the community I had helped to build. Would my clinic survive without me? And what was my next move? With these questions racing through my mind, I dozed fitfully, only to be awoken by the sound of the landing gear. "It's approximately three fifteen local time and fifty degrees Fahrenheit in New York City," our captain announced as we crawled into terminal four of JFK. "Welcome to America." As we started walking off the plane, I felt déjà vu. I thought of the scene in *Coming to America*, when the prince says to Akeem as they walk into the airport: "Remember, Akeem, no one here must know I am a royalty. I must act like the common man." I was a common man, but I had made it to the United States, the land of opportunity.

I followed the people heading toward the immigration officers, following the lines for visitors, which were long and slow compared to the line for citizens across the way from us. When it was my turn, I approached the officer box.

"What brings you to America?" he asked me. He was a big, imposing man, with a clean-shaven head and a look on his face that betrayed nothing. Since I had a visitor's visa, I said I came for a two-week vacation. The officer looked at my passport, looked up at me, and then stamped my passport. But then he lingered. He looked at me again and did not return my passport.

"Is everything okay?" I asked.

"You just need to undergo further inspection." He stepped out of the box. "This way, sir, please follow me," he said kindly.

There is a stark difference between a refugee and an asylum seeker. A refugee is someone outside their country who cannot return to their home country out of fear of persecution. An asylum seeker is a category of refugee who has newly arrived at the border of a country in which they hope to seek asylum. In America, asylum is a protection granted to people fleeing persecution under the United States Refugee Act of 1980. There are two categories of asylum: affirmative and defensive. Affirmative asylum seekers are already living in a host country when their home country's conditions change, leading them to seek protection in their host country. Defensive asylum seekers, such as I, arrive at the border asking for protection.

There is no guidebook for seeking asylum. Like many—if not most—refugees, I knew nothing about the asylum process before arriving at the border. I would soon learn how complicated the U.S. immigration system is by living through it.

I followed the officer into a small, air-conditioned, all-white room. He left without saying a further word. I waited alone for more than three hours; I'm sure I was exhibiting the characteristics of someone suffering a nervous breakdown.

Finally, a new, muscled officer walked in to escort me to baggage claim. I was confused. Did they think I would run into the airport? Where would I go? The bag claim room was empty, and I found my black bag easily, which the officer searched after returning me to the waiting room.

He found my birth certificate, bachelor's degree, and other documents. "Why are you bringing these with you on a vacation?" he asked.

I was too afraid to tell the truth. Was he the right person to discuss my immigration case with? He asked more questions: Do my parents live in the United States? Do I have any claim of being a U.S citizen, a parent or a child here? Have I ever tried to come into the U.S. before? What did I tell the consular in the U.S. embassy in Nigeria during my visa application? I could not have told the consular office I was coming to seek asylum when I applied for a visa—if I had done that, I would not have gotten a visa. Eventually, he concluded I would be returned to Nigeria and banned from entering the United States for a minimum of five to ten years. I had no other options at this point but to plead. "Sir," I said, "I cannot return to Nigeria. I will be killed for being gay."

The officer looked at me, and his countenance said he'd seen this before, that I was trying to trick him. "If you stay here," he replied, "we will have to take you to jail." I believed he said that to scare me or intimidate me into agreeing to leave.

I was suddenly unable to hold back my tears. "Sir, I don't want to go to jail."

"If you don't want to go to jail, then I think you should go back to your country." He insisted I sign the deportation papers, and at this point we were joined by a female officer. She explained, "If you do not sign the deportation papers, your case cannot be moved into removal proceedings. That is what gives you an opportunity to meet an immigration judge to decide your case."

Her tone was sympathetic and warm—but what if I signed the deportation papers in order to seek asylum, only to be returned to Nigeria? I had no life in Nigeria, I replied. I did not know how to explain all I had endured to get here, and found myself wondering why I was being threatened with imprisonment. I was frightened, tired, jet-lagged. But I had so few options that I took the leap of faith and signed my name. "You may call your family, if you'd like," the kind officer explained. But it was nearly one in the morning back home.

About 6:15 p.m., almost two hours after my plane had landed at terminal four, I sat close to the border patrol desk at JFK, waiting to be processed, when I heard the chant on television: *Build the wall! Build the wall!* I sat silently questioning if this was a movie or the news. I had arrived just a week before the monumental election between Hillary Clinton and Donald Trump. I did not know who Mr. Trump was and had perhaps only heard of him in passing. As I watched, what became clearer was my own naiveté. I believed America was welcoming of all people, and yet the crowd chanted louder and louder.

In a new room, the officers took my photo, fingerprinted me, and then locked me in a tiny holding cell. There was but one concrete slab to sit on, and a toilet, which I could smell as I tried to sleep. I lay on the concrete slab for more than two hours before two new officers arrived, opened the sliding door, and asked me to stand. I stood up, not knowing what to expect, when the female officer said, "Bring forth your hands." I was handcuffed and shackled by the feet.

How unjust this felt; I had come to this country seeking protection from danger, and there I was in chains. I could not help but remember the incident that made me flee Nigeria, hearing the chants of the angry mob singing behind my beating, "He is gay, we have found out!" I was so ashamed to think that people would believe me to be a criminal. The officer pushed me along, and I began to cry, regretting suddenly my decisions. I knew where this bus would take me without needing to be told. The officer opened the back door and pushed me in.

Since the Immigration Act of 1917, gay immigrants (or anyone considered to be a "pervert" or "deviant") had been excluded from the United States under blanket categories that shut out the "mentally or physically defective."* The Immigration and Nationality Act of 1952 preserved the exclusion, using new language: immigrants "afflicted with psychopathic personality" were barred from entering the United States. In 1959, George Fleuti, a gay immigrant from Switzerland, was ordered to be deported based on belonging to that category. He appealed his deportation on the grounds that "psychopathic personality" is a hopelessly vague term. The Ninth Circuit judge agreed, declaring the law "void for vagueness" in this case, and staying Fleuti's deportation order.

This ruling was a short-lived victory. The Immigration and Nationality Act of 1965 included language specifically intended to prevent queer people from entering the country: according to the American Bar Association, in reaction to Fleuti's case, the committee in charge of drafting the act "specifically included

* Suzanne Enzerink, "The 1917 Immigration Act that Presaged Trump's Muslim Ban," JSTOR Daily, April 12, 2017, https://daily.jstor.org/1917-immigration-law-presaged-trumps-muslim-ban/.

the term 'sexual deviation' as a ground of exclusion" in order "to resolve any doubt."*

The United Nations Refugee Convention of 1951 established that individuals with a "well-founded fear of being persecuted" based on membership of a "particular social group" are entitled to seek asylum abroad.†

Today, homosexuality is illegal in nearly seventy countries, and at the time of the 1951 convention, it was still illegal in Australia, the UK, most of the United States, and most of Europe—in Australia and other former British colonies, these laws were a legacy of British colonial rule. When the United States began accepting gay and lesbian asylum seekers in 1990, some states still had anti-sodomy laws on the books. (The Supreme Court ultimately declared these laws unconstitutional in 2003 with its decision in Lawrence v. Texas.) Even after legalizing homosexuality, some governments disputed LGBTQ asylum seekers' membership in the "particular social group" category, arguing that queer people are not a unified social group, or that they could simply hide their sexuality.

Queer identity is different from other persecuted identities: it often alienates individuals even from their immediate family, which is not usually true of people who belong to persecuted religious or political groups. This can make it difficult for queer asylum seekers to talk to anyone about their sexuality.

* Rosenberg, District Director, Immigration & Naturalization Service v. Fleuti, 374 U.S. 449 (1963), https://scholar.google.com/scholar_case?case=10467047861409373772&hl=en&as_sdt=6,33&as_vis=1.

† Convention Relating to the Status of Refugees, July 28, 1951, https://www.un.org/en/genocideprevention/documents/atrocity-crimes/Doc.23_convention%20refugees.pdf.

Even if you were to make it into the United States one way or another, your path might lead you to a detention center. The use of detention centers was suspended in America after World War II when the American government proclaimed it was inhumane to keep people seeking protection in a prison cell. It wasn't until 1966, when Australia opened the first modern migrant detention center, that they were reintroduced. In 1970, England opened their first dedicated migrant center: the Harmondsworth Immigration Removal Centre, with France shortly following. By 1981, when detention centers were once again normalized globally, former president Ronald Reagan reintroduced their use in the United States specifically for Haitian and Cuban refugees seeking asylum—they were largely considered by his administration to be unskilled, and therefore undesirable. President Ronald Reagan also launched a renewed War on Drugs that would pave the way for the increased militarization of border enforcement, conflating drug and immigration enforcement through interdiction programs. You might note this rhetoric—of certain immigrants being undesirable, as well as certain groups being responsible for a so-called War on Drugs—has sustained itself well into the modern Trump era.

When I arrived at the Elizabeth Detention Center in New Jersey in October of 2016, I did not know how long I would be staying. I was only informed I would get to meet with an asylum officer in seven days for a "credible fear" interview. Only then would an officer determine if I was eligible to make my plea before a judge or be returned to Nigeria. I was afraid of staying in a jail-like setting, where all detainees were assessed and divided up into three classifications: people who have a prior criminal history in orange uniforms; migrants apprehended at the border airports, southern border, and any entry point; and undocumented immigrants who are apprehended in the United States. I was given the standard blue jumpsuit for a level one detainee, who are considered the lowest threat of the three groups. I had seen these prison uniforms in movies before, but I did not ever imagine myself wearing one.

The Elizabeth Detention Center was situated in an abandoned warehouse in New Jersey, surrounded by old warehouses, with Newark airport within walking distance. At first I was placed in a holding cell for twenty-four hours, before finally being relocated to what was called the Gulf dorm, an open-floor plan with a total of forty-four beds, thirty-eight on the first floor and eight on the first deck, all made of concrete slabs with a mattress placed on top. I was given Bed 26. There were two televisions in our dorm, one for English speakers and one for Spanish speakers. Two steps from the television were our dining tables. Everything seemed to happen in one room—where we ate, slept, and used the bathroom.

I was told I would not be addressed by name, but instead by a nine-digit alien number. More commonly we were referred to by our bed number, and the detainees also used your bed number to reference you—not what I was used to. It became quickly obvious that Bed 26 was one of the worst beds in Gulf dorm, located directly in front of the dormitory toilets. Everyone in the dorm knew when someone was using the toilet, but the occupant of Bed 26 suffered during and after.

We did not have access to the outside world. The only natural light filtered in through a square opening in the roof, and when it snowed, our small square of sunlight was blocked. Despite the awful conditions, I knew I could not afford to return to Nigeria. I opted instead for patience.

The process of seeking asylum is always complex—but I was utterly alone in America. Worse yet, no one back home knew where I was, and I couldn't access my cell phone, which was taken from me before I entered the detention center. The calling cards from the center were very expensive. I worried about what my friends and family must have been thinking—where was I? Was I safe? I thought especially of my mother, who was then living alone in Warri, hoping I would return from Abuja one day to come live nearby. The little money I arrived with only lasted a few days, as I used it to buy calling cards so I could call around looking for an immigration lawyer and commissary.

I may not have been in any obvious immediate danger, but I was certainly homesick and in shock. Growing up, the America I had seen on TV was a place with less segregation, a place of acceptance. But this—a warehouse with mattresses on concrete slabs, with one square of sunlight—was how I found America treating those who came seeking its freedoms. I was now living through another version of America I had seen on TV—one populated by blue and orange jumpsuits. The stark difference began to set in as I made myself at home.

The first weekend of living in the detention center, I got to see the other West Africans' true colors. On Saturday afternoon after the head count, some of the guys asked the officer to tune in to the English premiership soccer game. It was a Chelsea game, and a Nigerian named Victor was a big Chelsea fan. I supported Arsenal, a rival London team, and did not want to get into any form of disagreement during my first week of living in the center.

I sat close to Victor in front of the TV and introduced myself, remarking that I hadn't seen or met him yet.

"Yes, I have been busy," he said. "I work in the kitchen, usually leave early in the morning, sleep on my bed in the afternoon, and attend religious services in the evenings."

"Are you new to this place?" I asked him.

"No," he said, somewhat solemnly. "I have been here for a long time." He turned to me. "Let us go to my bed and we can discuss more," he said politely.

Victor was in Bed 11, on the top right-hand side of the dorm. On his bed lay a Bible and a Catholic cross with Jesus on it. He had created his own altar right at the corner of his bed. It was then that I knew I would not tell him why I came to America. I was used to judging others before getting to know them.

Victor was arrested at the airport just like me, but he spent six months in an American prison for falsifying his entry documents before he was sent to the detention center to defend his deportation. I sat there speechless as he explained to me that, between his time in jail and transfer to detention, Victor had spent more than eleven months in a confined system for fleeing persecution in Nigeria. He told me that working in the kitchen and watching soccer were the only sources of relief he had after leaving his daughter behind in Nigeria.

He smiled at me, looking happy despite the horrific experience he had just relayed. He continued, "I had more breathing room in the prison compared to this facility. In this building, we don't go out even for a minute a day." He was brutally honest in his introduction to life in the center. He looked at me and said, "I do not want to scare you, by any means. I just want you to know what you are getting into and be prepared for the long haul."

Victor pointed to another bed, where a guy was sleeping during the day as folks screamed at the television for their teams to win. "That guy is called 'Shampoo,'" he told me, "because he hoards all the shampoo to have a long bath." He was from Burkina Faso and had been in detention for more than thirteen months, with no progress in his case. Worst of all, he spoke little English and often kept to himself. On and on Victor told me stories of people at the center, pointing to different beds, explaining each of their plights. And then, he looked at me and said, "some of the people you see today, you won't see them by morning."

"Where do they go?" I asked.

"People get deported every day. We wake up with new people in their beds. It's just the reality of this place. You might not see me tomorrow."

"I cannot return to Nigeria," I told him. "If I lose my case, I'd rather remain locked up here and keep fighting than return to my death."

"You should come work in the kitchen with me, then," he said. "To make some money."

I spent these first few days getting to know people, waking up to have breakfast, and then going back to bed to sleep off the jetlag. I joined the guys in the gym, but usually only watched television while the guys worked out. I got joy from playing video games for an hour, or at the library where I read up on asylum. At this point, I did not know what awaited me. I was going to take each day as it came.

As I stated earlier, your name is replaced with a nine-digit alien number when you arrive at the detention center. After seven days, I had lost my name and my sense of time. I became disoriented. The food had no taste. And it stung each time an officer called me by my bed number rather than my name. But after a week, I was called for my credible fear interview.

This interview determines if you are eligible to see a judge or if you will be immediately returned home.

The officer started the interview by reading a long statement to me: "The purpose of this interview is to determine if you may be eligible for asylum or protection from removal to a country where you fear persecution or torture. I am going to ask you a question on why you fear returning to a country or any other country you may be removed to." The officer's tone was dead serious. I had questions, but I kept silent.

"Do you have an attorney?" she asked.

"No," I replied. "I have contacted an organization, but I haven't received a response on representation."

"Would you like to proceed today without an attorney?"

"Yes," I replied.

Her next question was totally unexpected.

"How did you know John Adewoye?" John was someone we called "Papa," an LGBTQ activist from Nigeria who was also a former priest that got humiliated and chased out of the church because they found out he was a member of the LGBTQ community. He now lives in Chicago, where he is an LGBTQ activist. I had found him through his story I read online and contacted him on Facebook between Cairo and New York. I realized this meant the officers had gone through my social media accounts.

"John is an LGBTQ activist," I replied. "But I don't know him personally."

"Do you work for him?" she asked.

"No," I replied. She moved on from there to more mundane questions, like had I ever been to the United States, to more complicated ones like: When did you realize you were gay?

"Since secondary school," I replied. "Since 2002. I was found touching a boy and it was brought to the attention of my school authorities. My parents had taken me to a traditional healer to fix me, but I am still gay. I have suffered persecution for being gay. That's why I came to the United States."

At this point, I had hidden my sexuality for a long time. I did not know how to talk about my relationship with other men because I had constantly dissociated myself from my reality. I had to tell a stranger my sexual life and the abuse I encountered in Abuja. She countered with an argument: anyone could walk into this country and claim they are gay, seeking protection. Why should we believe you?

In some sense, she was right—I had hidden the private details of my love life for so long that I favored being vague. Besides, I worried about what would happen if this didn't work out—if the government returned me to Abuja, would they have to disclose to the Nigerian government that I was gay? I told her how I came out to my grandmother, my first love Bobby. About my work in Abuja, and the people I left behind. I pleaded with her—"Ma'am, I am educated. I have a family, and a life. I had ambitions. If I could pursue them freely in Nigeria, I would have stayed."

Apparently she was satisfied, or out of questions, as she picked up a piece of paper and read from it. "You stated that you identify as gay, and you advocated for LGBTQ+ rights in Nigeria. You were beaten by homophobic members of your community because of your sexual orientation and advocacy. You could not report the assault to the police, because you would be imprisoned, as same-sex relationships, cohabitation, and LGBTQ+ advocacy is criminalized in Nigeria. Recently, your name was posted on the LGBTQ+ advocacy website as someone recognized for advocating for the health rights of men having sex with men. If you go back, you will be arrested and imprisoned by the government because of your sexual orientation and advocacy; and you will be harmed and killed by a homophobic society." She paused.

"Is that correct?" she asked.

"Yes," I replied.

More than an hour into the process, her face remained unmoving. It seemed nothing I said had pierced her. Her gaze was daring, trying to weed out any lies. After some time, she stood up. "You can return to your room. That is all for today. You'll hear from us soon."

I returned to Bed 26 and waited, seven days exactly, until an envelope arrived on November 10, 2016. Inside was a letter from the officer: they had determined my claim was valid. The letter said that the above captioned case had been scheduled for a MASTER hearing before the immigration court on December 5, 2016 at eight thirty a.m. I would get to meet with an immigration judge in just under a month. Now I would need a lawyer to represent me.

* * *

If seeking asylum in America—or around the world—is already a difficult process, both psychologically and emotionally, things were certainly made more challenging by being gay. As an LGBTQ person, there were so few people I could relate to at the detention center. The likelihood of danger within a detention center is staggeringly higher for LGBTQ persons. We face a greater risk of being molested sexually; transgender asylum seekers are constantly misgendered, not only in speech but in their dorm assignments; and of course, there are religious extremists even within detention centers. These factors made being "out" in the detention center quite difficult, if not outright dangerous. Worse yet, LGBTQ detainees fear reporting incidents to detention center staff and management for fear of retaliation. LGBTQ people seeking asylum often remain unrecognized and invisible in the asylum system unless they specifically come forward and out themselves. This is particularly difficult for those who are reluctant to come out due to their specific life situations (i.e., family, marriage, community), feelings of shame and fear to talk about their sexuality/gender identity, and/or a lack of safe accommodations and other spaces that would allow for a "coming out."

In Gulf dorm, there were about six other Africans. We naturally gravitated toward one another, but that meant asking each other questions—about who we were, and why we had come here. After my credible fear interview, though I wanted to keep details about myself as private as I could, I realized that was forcing myself back into another closet. I tried to be forthright and honest when I was asked what brought me to America. I told them I came to seek asylum because I am gay; they did not respond kindly. One of them said to me, "You are lying."

"Why would I lie to you?" I asked.

My intention in telling them was simply to be honest. I had hoped that I might find another community member who was also seeking protection because of their sexuality. They might help me understand the process better and give me a sense of what to expect for LGBTQ people seeking asylum.

But this man had never met a gay person before me. He believed homosexuality was a myth. Those African men told others in the center that I was gay and some of the Spanish guys started calling me *maricón*. I did not know *maricón* was a derogatory term for gay people in Spanish. Perhaps I should not have been so open about who I was, but I had hoped to be met with understanding, with kindness. After all, we had all came to a new country to seek protection from discrimination or danger, or both. Yet I felt like I was reliving my life in Nigeria, fearful to express myself, and when people spoke to me, I grew unsure if they were joking around or insulting. It was not in my nature to be quiet, but I tried to stay quiet and keep to myself, fearing that people would take my conversations as sexual advances. I loved watching soccer, but I feared that arguing about our favorite teams would lead to them telling me I didn't know about *men's games*. I also worried about consequences more drastic than social isolation—in American TV jails, I had heard about rape. I tried to take showers alone, so people couldn't falsely accuse me of sexual advances. When I could not shower alone, other men would mock me by pretending to have sex with each other. It became a waking nightmare simply to eat or watch TV. No one wanted to be seen socializing with a gay man.

Soon after, I met Jenny. She was a transgender asylum seeker from Honduras who also faced harassment in the detention center. Jenny was introverted and shy, but flamboyantly expressive in her mannerisms as a woman. She had been living in Florida and suffered a head injury when she was pushed down two flights of stairs by her boyfriend. While in the hospital, she was caught by ICE and deported before she could see a judge. When she fled Honduras again, she was detained at the same detention center I was. Though Jenny identified as female, she was brought to the male-only Gulf dorm, where she faced harsh treatment, especially from the West Africans who didn't understand what it meant to be transgender, and the other Spanish folks did not have the patience to explain things to her.

I tried to be a close friend to Jenny—here, I thought, I finally had an ally in someone who understood what queer oppression felt like. But Jenny only spoke Spanish.

Still, I tried to look for ways to be a friend to her and support her at the center. I was always struck by her caring nature—if an insect got in her way, she'd jump past it instead of killing it. The line for morning breakfast could be very long and aggressive. I would run to the front of the line to save a spot for Jenny because her walk was very tender. But she was surrounded by men who behaved like animals. I didn't want her to starve because the guys usually rushed the line, so I would get two plates and gather food for the both of us. The officers were aware I was taking two pieces of food for Jenny and me, but they mostly left us alone. We tried using visuals to communicate, but it was difficult, so our meals were usually quiet. We would smile at each other, and sometimes I would chat with the others around us.

Still, I could see in Jenny the same loneliness of isolation that I felt growing within me. I would use my money from working in the kitchen to buy us extra food without asking her. She would look at me and smile. It might have seemed like we were dating, but I just felt a genuine kinship with her, as someone from my community. As a gay person, you reach a point where you develop an armor around yourself out of necessity.

When I wasn't with Jenny, I was watching soccer or playing volleyball with the other men while she'd nap. During church in the evenings, Jenny would sit at the back of the chapel with Charlie, another newly arrived trans detainee. They were both reserved and quiet, but they both spoke Spanish, which I think was a much-needed comfort.

I learned of another trans detainee who was not shy like Jenny and would often join her dorm mates on the volleyball court. Her courage and outgoing nature were derided by the Africans in my dorm, who would say nasty things about her, even going so far as to joke they'd rape her at night. If I had come all this way in search of a better life for myself, how could I sit idly by while hearing threats such as these? The courage to be out as a gay person is to be comfortable with who you are. For me, I found my courage in not wanting Bobby and Emmanuel's deaths to be in vain. I did not come this far to give up now. Despite the persecution, I knew I would be out of this place one day and be able to live my life, but I did not want to live a lie anymore, or watch another community member go through such humiliation.

I started speaking more to the West Africans about gender identity and LGBTQ rights, emboldened by the friendship I had forged with Jenny, and their displays of ignorance. I worried

I sounded defensive, but I was unapologetic, and to my surprise most people were eager to learn more. My peers were not only interested in learning about LGBTQ people, but about the asylum process as well. I read up on asylum and immigration laws and tried to explain them to the folks around me. When they had questions about the process, they began coming to me. The people who felt I was overbearing started calling me the "noisemaker." It was a name I wore with pride—I was glad to be known for challenging injustice in any and all forms within the dorm.

My fellow African detainees weren't all bigots, by any stretch of the imagination. I became great friends with Mohammed and Mzee, two Tanzanians in their thirties. They had never been to America before, like me, and spoke Swahili. Mzee had muscles like a gym bunny, and though Mohammed liked going to the gym, he was more prudent. We quickly became friends, bonding over discussions about our families back home. Mohammed had a daughter a few months before he fled his home to the United States. His wife and daughter were back home, and he prayed for them daily, hoping he could bring them to America one day. As we got closer, I explained why it was important to be a "noisemaker," and to my surprise, he was kind and empathetic as he listened and encouraged me to continue standing up for what was right.

Soon, Mohammed and Mzee began asking me to help them handwrite letters in English to their American pen pals. This was an amazing novelty to me.

"Mohammed," I asked him. "How do you have a pen pal?"

He laughed. "Mr. Edafe," as he called me in his very formal way. "There is an organization, called First Friends of New Jersey and New York," he explained. A fellow Tanzanian in the Delta dorm had introduced him to them.

"Who are they?" I asked.

He explained that the First Friends were Americans who volunteered by visiting with folks in detention centers, and by writing them letters. They were working toward building communities for new immigrants arriving in America, like us, who only had some understanding of English, and often no community of their own. So of course I helped them with their letters; I was honored to be of service to these two beautiful, kindhearted men.

Mohammed's pen pal was Flora from New Jersey. She regularly wrote him letters which he brought to me to read and to help him reply to.

Dear Flora, I'd write for him. *I hope your day is good . . .*

"Why not 'good morning' or 'afternoon'?" Mohammad would ask. I had to explain the use of broad strokes in English. "Because you don't know the time of the day Flora receives her mail," I said.

Flora bought Mohammad a children's coloring book, with descriptions of English words: *A for Apple* and *Z for Zebra*. We also learned greetings and mannerisms: "Good morning, Ma," or "Good morning, Sir." In Swahili, there are no separate words for "he" and "her," so pronouns were the hardest for him to learn. Gradually, I began to teach him English so that one day he might respond on his own. He was confused but sweet, and open to learning. Over the next few weeks, he came back to me with new sentences using "he" and "her," trying to impress me that he had finally mastered pronouns.

Mohammed told me I should call the First Friends of New Jersey and New York—perhaps they could help me with my case, he thought. He stood by my side while I anxiously placed the call. A lady from First Friends picked up the call and told me I would be visited by a friend from First Friends, but that they didn't provide legal help. As an LGBTQ asylum seeker, they suggested putting me in touch with Immigration Equality, another organization that helped with the legal aspects of immigration. After some phone calls, I found myself talking to a paralegal who promised they'd share my message with the team, and someone would call soon. When a call never arrived, I remained persistent.

I called Immigration Equality regularly because they had a toll-free line. After relaying more of my story to the paralegal, she was able to connect me to a law firm that decided to represent me pro bono. I would meet with them in a month's time, and we would begin working on clearing my path to freedom.

I was elated on the day I was set to meet the team from Debevoise and Plimpton, a Manhattan law firm representing my case and assisting with the asylum documents to file in court. I was jittery, moving from one table to another through the dorm, talking to as many people as I could. I tried to find folks who had met with lawyers before, to know how I should prepare. Folks at the center did not like my inquisitive nature. They had learned to be cautious of others. We would hear rumors of ICE and USCIS planting detainees to listen to conversations as informants. Very few would give me real answers to my questions, except for Jean from Burkina Faso, but his English wasn't very good. He told me to calm down, that all would be fine.

The day I met my legal team, I wore a new white undershirt and new white socks, trying to look my best. Around eleven a.m., I was called in by a detention officer, who walked me to the visitation room.

Eventually, two lawyers arrived, and the officer escorted us to a private room. The first lawyer had golden-blond hair pulled back from her face. She introduced herself as Mrs. Ross. She was not an immigration lawyer but a corporate lawyer who had heard about my case and wanted to help. Though she was a bit reserved, she had a sunny demeanor that made opening up to her very easy. The other lawyer was named Emilie, an Asian American woman with an embracing persona. She was the same height as Mrs. Ross, but wore a black suit and clear glasses, which framed her dark eyelashes and smoky eyeshadow each time she blinked. Without saying much—just exchanging a few pleasantries and kind gestures—I felt in good hands.

"We've heard about your story from Immigration Equality," Mrs. Ross said, before pausing to ask, "Are you okay?"

"Yes," I replied, though I hardly was.

"You look a bit beaten-up," she said.

"No, no, far from it," I reassured her. "I'm okay. I am just excited to meet both of you." I knew nothing about the asylum process except what I had read, so I was willing to stay quiet and allow them to do their magic.

For a moment the room was silent, and I sensed an unease about how to proceed. Perhaps they worried their questions might offend me. I was worried that maybe other folks in the center could overhear our conversation, and what I was disclosing.

"So," Mrs. Ross said. "Why don't you tell us about yourself and what made you come to seek asylum in America?"

I couldn't help but feel this was starting to become redundant. However, I explained again the circumstances that brought me to this meeting room. The lawyers were forthright: they had never taken an asylum case before; I would be their first. Mrs. Ross told me she was a lesbian, so it was important to her to support another gay person who came to America in need of help. It cheered me to know Mrs. Ross understood why I had fled to America.

The lawyers treated me with dignity; they called me by my name. They reassured me that I was courageous for fleeing danger and offered to represent my asylum case before the immigration judge.

I did not know if I was allowed to hug her or shake her hands. We laughed together, sitting in that room. I knew they were ready to fight for me, and they both left no stone unturned regarding my case before they left.

In December 2016, it was finally time for me to meet with a judge. Before this, my only experience in a courthouse was signing affidavits for my birth certificate in 2002, the year I began secondary school.

The courtroom was located in the same building as the detention center. Immigration court is different from normal courthouses; it's typically a small space consisting of the judge's bench, tables for the defense and prosecution, and pews, where I sat, with two empty rows for friends and family to observe the proceedings, though I had no one with me.

"Edafe Okporo," the judge called. She was a stark woman with brown hair, unsmiling. I had been told by other detainees that the judge was very harsh, and that meetings with her often resulted in longer stays at the center. Most notably, though, she wasn't wearing the large wig that Nigerian and British judges often wore, which perhaps made her seem normal and less intimidating.

"Yes, my lord," I responded, as we say in Nigeria.

She laughed and said, "In America, you say 'Your Honor.'" She waited to make sure I understood before continuing on. "You are among the gay men from Nigeria," she stated, rather than asking.

"Yes, Your Honor," I replied, and we both laughed. That question would have made me shy in the past, but no longer. It was the truth.

"And will you be representing yourself?"

"No, Your Honor," I replied. "I am speaking with my lawyers—they'd like me to pick up the asylum form and I would like them to be at my next hearing."

She then handed me an asylum form that my lawyers would help me fill out and return on my second court date in a week.

She had no further questions. "You can now leave my court," she said, not unkindly.

For all that lead-up to this moment, it was rather quick. I left the courtroom with optimism. I'd heard from other detainees that they might wait as much as three months between hearing dates; I was encouraged to learn my hearing would be just a week later. Yet until then, I returned to the detention center.

The time I spent in the detention center was the most challenging in my life. Apart from the initial harassment I faced, being far from home, jailed in a new country, learning to sleep in a room with many strangers, I found that I had unlimited time but nothing to do with it. Our routines were pretty stable. We were required to stand at our beds every four hours for staff to count heads, which could sometimes take up to an hour. We had regularly scheduled volleyball sessions, gym time, and even video games. But we never saw the outside world. The closest we came was the big opening in the roof of the volleyball court, where sunlight, rain, and snow would filter through. The center was located near Newark airport. How trying to see planes flying overhead through our little skylight, filled with people able to come and go as they pleased, a reminder of the freedom of the outside world. By contrast, I was locked up in a warehouse, having lost my freedom in pursuit of it. The noisy planes, after a few days, became something like a lullaby.

Like most prisons, our detention center was run by a private company, profiting off the jailing of immigrants. These facilities are traded on the stock market, and those who run them do whatever they can to cut costs and improve efficiencies to be more profitable. For example, food was a sunk cost (money that was already spent and accounted for) but health care was not, and therefore, was very poor. According to reports from the

*Washington Post** and CNN,† the number one cause of death in U.S. immigration facilities is lack of access to quality health care services. But the overall cost of running the centers themselves is cheap—us, the detainees, ran the facility. I worked in the kitchen, four hours each day, preparing lunch for the dormitory. Those of us working in the kitchen ate there, and cleaned the plates, as well as the kitchen and toilets. Though I worked from ten thirty a.m. until two thirty p.m. each day, this was still considered "voluntary work," and we were paid just a dollar a day into our commissary accounts.

Our current immigration system is not functioning as it was set out to be. According to U.S. immigration policy, when an asylum seeker is detained, after seven days of detainment they are supposed to meet with an asylum officer who would determine the credibility of their asylum claim. After this step, if their claim for asylum is credible, they would be eligible for parole, to live in America and fight for their case outside of the detention center. However, I was denied parole due to the immigration system classifying me as a flight risk. This struck me as somewhat unrealistic—I had fled already to America, for protection; where else would I run to? Not granting asylum seekers parole and alternatives to detention is partially to prolong their stay at the

* Patricia Sullivan, "Report: Half of Recent Immigrant Detainee Deaths Due to Inadequate Medical Care," *Washington Post*, June 20, 2018, https://www.washingtonpost.com/local/immigration/report-half-of-recent-immigrant-detainee-deaths-due-to-inadequate-medical-care/2018/06/19/fe313670-73df-11e8-b4b7-308400242c2e_story.html.

† Meera Senthilingam, "Half of Recent Immigrant Detainee Deaths Due to Inadequate Medical Care, Report Finds," CNN, June 20, 2018, https://www.cnn.com/2018/06/20/health/immigrant-detainee-deaths-medical-care-bn/index.html.

detention centers, profiting from asylum seekers in the privately run prison system. Because the private detention center groups trade in the U.S stock market, immigrant families and children being locked up in prison are being traded by the United States capitalist system as commodities. Yet I feel that promoting this culture of punishing migrants seeking protection in America is un-American. We cannot be a beacon of hope and yet dehumanize people seeking protection at the same time; there should be an oversight of the detention centers where migrants are kept, a separate watchdog or community set up to inspect the center from time to time. Though in general, I feel that the United States should stop using private prison to hold up immigrants altogether.

Many countries do not use detention for migrants—for example, our Canadian neighbors provide housing for people seeking asylum. When I visited the Netherlands in 2018, I saw that they used the same system of government-provided housing and monthly stipends for asylum seekers. There are suitable alternatives to detention, such as parole and bonds—bonds are monies paid into the U.S immigration system. If the person misses their case, they get deported and lose the money they have paid. Bond fees usually cost around $1,500, but under the Trump administration, they ranged from an average of $12,500 to $17,000.* Even if bond inflation was rectified, other alternatives, like ankle monitor bracelets for immigrants living outside detention centers, could reduce flight risk. Alternatives such as

* Daniel Bush, "Under Trump, Higher Immigration Bonds Mean Longer Family Separations," *PBS NewsHour*, June 28, 2018, https://www.pbs.org/newshour/politics/under-trump-higher-immigration-bonds-mean-longer-family-separations.

these would reduce the number of people locked away in private prisons and detention centers.

But under the current system, the more people imprisoned the better, since these prisons generate profits for their billionaire owners, and are used as a bargaining chip by lobbyists and politicians. Yet alternatives such as parole, bonds, and location monitors are not only more ethical, but cheaper. Detention centers are largely funded by taxpayers—and we pay an average of $201 per day, per person, with up to 50,000 people detained each day in America.* The country is bleeding money to keep immigrants locked up—it seems only right as taxpayers that we should have a say in whether we want to build a more humane immigration system that doesn't directly enhance the wealth of their private owners.

In addition to the financial benefits, one of the many reasons why this system seems to thrive is because it is deeply embedded within a white supremacist framework—the system is designed to deter Black and brown people from entering America. Profit happens to be a bonus. The financial and ethical dilemmas notwithstanding, asylum law is quite complicated—perhaps by design. Asylum seekers without legal representation are more likely to say things that will incriminate themselves and lead them to lose their cases. It is essential for asylum seekers to get representation from the government, or at the very least, a liaison to explain the process. If a U.S. citizen gets arrested, they have a right to a lawyer; it seems only just that would-be U.S. citizens

* Jaden Urbi, "This Is How Much It Costs to Detain an Immigrant in the U.S.," CNBC, June 20, 2018, https://www.cnbc.com/2018/06/20/cost-us-immigrant-detention-trump-zero-tolerance-tents-cages.html.

should be afforded those same resources. Asylum seekers who are detained without lawyers have lower chances of getting the protection they need. Access to legal representation increases the chances of people seeking protection to get the help they need.* Universal representation of all asylum seekers who arrive at the U.S border would not only make it easier for people fleeing persecution but would also shorten the wait time at the detention centers, which averages approximately 156 days.† We have seen shorter wait times in the New York/New Jersey area after 2015, when New York State offered free legal counsel in three counties, and in 2019, when the city offered representation to asylum seekers who arrived in New York. In September 2020, the New York City Mayor's Office of Immigrant Affairs provided money to organizations offering free legal representation to asylum seekers.‡ Since the program started, there has been a sharp decline in the amount of asylum seekers that do not get their asylum claims filed properly, reduction in wait times for a pro bono lawyer, and better understanding among asylum seekers of their rights to asylum. Until this process is made more equitable,

* Trac Immigration, *Record Number of Asylum Cases in FY 2019* (report date: January 8, 2020), https://trac.syr.edu/immigration/reports/588/.

† Monsy Alverado et al., "'These People Are Profitable': Under Trump, Private Prisons Are Cashing In on ICE Detainees," *USA Today*, December 19, 2019, https://www.usatoday.com/in-depth/news/nation/2019/12/19/ice-detention-private-prisons-expands-under-trump-administration/4393366002/.

‡ NYC Mayor's Office of Immigrant Affairs, "ActionNYC: Mayor's Office of Immigrant Affairs Announces Funding Awards to Organizations Providing Free and Safe Immigration Legal Services to New Yorkers Citywide," September 30, 2020, https://www1.nyc.gov/site/immigrants/about/press-releases/moia-announces-funding-awards-to-organizations-09-30-2020.page.

most asylum seekers must rely on the countless organizations fighting to make America a better place by filling in gaps in the process created by the federal government. Across all fifty states, legal organizations are donating their time, effort, and energy toward representing asylees and fighting against harsh policies that hinder people seeking protection in America.

At the beginning of my stay, I had plenty of time to consider my circumstances. I still missed home and my family. I thought often about my beloved Mrs. Alice. I thought about my mother, whom I wanted to speak with more than anyone. Calls to Africa were expensive, and even still, if she did pick up, she'd be greeted by a prompt informing her that "this call is from the Elizabeth Detention Center," or "Correction Corps of America." Nigerian culture credits "difficult children" to their mothers, and being jailed certainly qualified as "difficult"; if my mum thought I was in jail in America, she would surely be ashamed and distraught. Despite all that I missed, it remained clear that I could not return. I did sometimes regret my decision—I had, up until this point, essentially forfeited my freedom for the sake of staying alive. But if I hadn't—would I be free, really? Or alive? I would have been forced into my shell, to listen to my parents' advice to find a nice woman to marry and start a family. Someone my age in America might be completing college or a master's degree, starting their first job, or traveling abroad. Perhaps I could have been doing any of those things back home. It seemed I could not win—I was not really free in Nigeria, and yet here I was, twenty-six years old and detained in America.

To avoid creating turmoil in my family, I decided to banish the idea of contacting them, for now at least. I dreamed of the day I would call my mum from outside the walls of the detention center, to triumphantly tell her I'd made it to America.

The one thing I held tightly to from my past life was my Christian faith. Stories from the Bible suddenly held new meaning and made more sense. I thought of Joseph, who went from prison to becoming a member of the king's entourage. I remembered Job, who lost everything, and got it back threefold.

Days and nights flew by, as I read my Bible, and went to the gym with Mzee and Mohammed, hoping against hope I would be out of the detention center in a few days' time.

As my asylum case proceeded through the court, the days and months added up. By the end of December 2016, I had been detained for a total of two months and one week, and my final hearing was finally scheduled—but not in a weeks' time; instead, I'd have to wait until the first week of March 2017. I began writing Bible verses on my case file:

Galatians 3:11: *The just shall live by faith.*

Jeremiah 1:8: *Be not afraid of their faces; for I am with thee to deliver thee, saith the LORD.*

Luke 21:13: *And it shall turn to you for a testimony.*

Even as the date approached and I tried to remain positive, I was met with more and more delays—the judge pushed my hearing from March to April. This would mean eight more weeks in the detention center. Even worse, the new date was four days before Mrs. Ross's wedding in Texas. Though I had five lawyers working with me, by now Mrs. Ross had become a close friend and ally. As a lesbian, she understood my suffering as a gay man.

"Don't lose hope," she told me over the phone, delivering the news. A few days later, some postcards arrived from her with pictures of New York City just across the river. For her, I would try.

After we hung up, I returned to my bed. The officer in the dorm that day was a Jamaican lady, one of the friendliest officers at the detention center. Seeing that I was obviously dispirited, she touched my shoulder and said, "Cheer up, man."

I told her about my delayed court date, the news, and she said: "You are not the first one and you are not going to be the last." She squeezed my shoulder. "Go take a shower with the water all the way up, and cry. Nobody will see your tears but you," she said. "It is okay to let out your emotions."

In my eight weeks of waiting, I began to think more about what my life would be like if I was granted protection. I had never been to New York, but I dreamed of it. It was the most popularly known city in my life abroad, after all. The sparse decorations that lined the walls of the detention center's visitation room included posters of the Statue of Liberty, the Brooklyn Bridge, and the Manhattan skyline. I dreamed of living in a skyscraper, seeing these places up close as though they might allow me to be more fully myself.

I killed time by joining Mzee and Mohammed at the gym some days, but instead of working out I often just watched the soccer games on television. Through First Friends, I had gained a pen pal named Lilian, who visited on occasion, and I wrote to her about my court case delay. Her responses were like meditations—writing to me about the sea, the sky, and finding calmness in my breath. I treasured her letters for the peace they brought me.

During my waiting period, Mohammed and Mzee received their final court dates too: Mzee's was to be April 17, and Mohammed's April 19. We were all assigned the same judge, Mr. Morrison, and would all hopefully leave the center around the same time. Mohammed and I spent most of our time together chatting about the possibility of renting a room in New York. We were optimistic, but tensions were high; I would turn back to the Bible then, and Mohammed would pray with me. It was a long, agonizing eight weeks of excruciating anxiety thinking what would be the outcome if I got my asylum, where would I live in America, would I be able to get a job? But nothing was concrete because it was all speculative thinking. A possibility for a future that was unknown and hanging in the balance of a judge's acceptance or rejection of my claim for asylum.

Some good news came in the form of a call from Mrs. Ross, who would be able to attend my hearing before heading to Texas for her wedding. She came in for a prep interview and brought another lawyer who had been working on my case, Mr. Grossman, to act as a prosecutor just to try me out before the main hearing. We took on a question-and-answer format of conversation that reminded me of my days on the debate team with Gloria.

Finally April 18, 2017, arrived. I woke with a pit in my stomach, a mix of nerves and excitement. There was always a risk of deportation back to Nigeria. But, win or lose, I would remain in America for now. If I had lost my case, I would challenge the decision in an appeal court. It was the difference between walking freely, safely, or remaining in a jail cell.

An officer arrived to collect me. As we walked down the rows of beds, the other guys clapped and cheered. Mohammed said he would pray for me. I was taken to a holding room and waited. When my lawyers arrived, I was shocked to see Mr. Kent, my American friend who worked for the U.S. government in Nigeria. My lawyers were in contact with him and he was willing to testify as a witness to the brutality suffered by me and LGBTQ Nigerians. Kent was supposed to be in South Africa for his work with the government, but his flight was delayed, so he decided to join me that morning. He was indeed a good man—and a good friend, which is what I needed in that moment.

Kent called me *nong*, a Thai name that means "younger brother."

"You will be out of here soon, *nong*," he told me with a soft smile. He had been a true elder brother to me and would often send me letters about American football, and even once, a postcard from the mountains in Switzerland. Winning my case that day meant I could return to the world with people like Kent: family I was beginning to make on my own.

After they left the waiting room for the court, I held my hands in prayer. Beyond a heavy, bounded metal gate, all I could see was an empty hallway to the courthouse. I was alone, anxious, pacing, counting to see how many steps filled the entire room when the officer called me—by my bed number—and asked me to follow him inside the courthouse.

In the courtroom, I sat close to my attorneys. The state prosecutor sat across the large table, Judge Morrison joined on a screen, dialing in virtually from Connecticut. Judge Morrison asked me to stand up and swear an affidavit that everything I said was the truth, the whole truth, and nothing but the truth, so help me God. The judge made mention of my friend, Mr. Kent, a witness for the case who would provide master testimony. I wanted to celebrate, but inside the courthouse I had to remain quiet.

The judge asked Mrs. Ross to begin the witness testimony.

"What is your name and where are you from?" she asked first. The questions progressed from easy answers—my name was Edafe Okporo and I was from Warri, Nigeria—to questions that took more consideration. Why did I flee? Why wasn't I safe in Nigeria.

I replied, "Mrs. Ross, the safest place I could live in Nigeria was Abuja," and then I explained that was where I had been attacked by a mob at my apartment.

"When you were attacked, why did you not go to your family?" she asked. I explained my relationship with my family was complicated, not to mention that the laws in Nigeria criminalized family members who support their gay son, punishable by ten years in prison.

The goal was to convince the judge that I was in peril—and would remain in peril unless I could stay in America. The questions may sound simple, but the stakes were anything but. This judge would have only two hours to decide my fate.

Mrs. Ross continued, asking me why I could not come out in Nigeria as a gay man. Why did I hide my sexuality? Was I successful at doing so? This part was easy.

I became tense again, however, when they asked me to describe the night of my attack in 2016. I did not want to appear weak in court, but I could not hide the shame and pain that besieged me having to relive that night.

I asked for a break. I told my lawyer I was holding back tears, that I did not want to cry in front of the judge and look like I was begging for sympathy. But Mrs. Ross told me this judge had seen all sort of cases and that I was doing okay so far.

When we resumed after my break, Mrs. Ross again asked me to recount that night. This would be the first time I had retold it.

I said, "I did not want to leave my country. I always wanted to fit in, but the law made it hard for me to fit in. My friends died of AIDS. If I did not fight, it could be me next. I came to America for many reasons, the attack being one of them. The night of the attack, I was overburdened by the fear I had to live with. It was my twenty-sixth birthday and I would never forget it."

I recounted the mob, their chanting my name outside. The words they called me. The way they dragged me into the street. I felt newly terrified retelling the story. You could hear a pin drop in the courtroom by the end. Mrs. Ross looked at me and gave a reassuring nod, not betraying any emotion herself.

"Thank you," she said. "And how did you escape from Nigeria? How did you secure the funds to escape?" I was somewhat stunned to be asked this—it seemed almost obvious to me, but Mrs. Ross wanted to leave no stone unturned. Before we arrived at court, she had submitted these documents to the judge and state prosecutor. After a particular question, Mrs. Ross would pause and present evidence, which included: a written declaration from me, the Same-Sex Marriage (Prohibition) Act of 2013, the fliers in the community calling for my death, medical reports of the attack and the injuries I sustained, letters of support from friends, my profile on Grindr, pictures of me and my past partners, and an affidavit from Kent.

The prosecutor looked at the stack of evidence in front of her.

She turned the pages one after the other, simultaneously staring at me. She flipped through and would stop at a page and stare straight at me for a while. She began asking nearly all of the same questions, but in different patterns, to see if I had lied or made anything up. I felt stripped open, searched inside and out.

The testimony lasted for up to an hour.

Then Mr. Kent testified on the conditions facing gay men in Nigeria. The judge thanked him for coming in that day. After my testimony and Kent's, the state prosecutor stated they did not have a case against me. If I was granted asylum, the state would not appeal the judge's decision. The court officer asked me to stand up and leave, and I returned to the waiting room. Everything was working in my favor. Still, I bit my fingernails, I fidgeted, I paced for probably an hour. That was when the officer returned, smiling.

Back in the courtroom, I sat down with Mrs. Ross, who was also smiling. She whispered, "I think they are granting."

I just sat, perplexed and a bit numb. I had learned not to get too hopeful by now.

"Edafe Okporo, please rise," the judge said. "Thank you for your bravery and courage. I am granting you permission to live in America."

Life is full of big and small moments—some joyous, some terrible. Yet thinking back to this day always brings a smile to my face—and a couple of tears. Those nine words. We were all so happy.

As we left the courtroom, Mrs. Ross said, "There have been nights and days of hard work, countless reviews, and some prayers for you to get released . . . and here you are, minutes away from walking out this door." I hugged her; she was not only my lawyer but also a friend. I thanked Mr. Kent for his support. I was a bit flustered realizing, first, that I would be leaving the center, and second, that I didn't know where I'd go next. Kent was returning to South Africa, so that ruled him out, and I couldn't impose on my lawyers anymore. It was unclear if Mohammed would be released and if we could get a place to live together like we'd discussed—but then again, I had no job, no income. Perhaps I could call Sylvester, my old roommate from Abuja who was living in the States now? I realized I was woefully uneducated on what would happen next—would the government provide a place for me to live? But I knew better than to ask the court further questions, or to push my luck.

Back in my dorm, folks were waiting for me to come and tell them what happened. We had a system in place—if someone raised their hands, they had won their case. I walked slowly through the halls, feeling the intensity of everyone's eyes on me. Then, I raised my hands. The room burst into cheers, congratulating me with whoops and hollers as I made my way back to my bed. Mohammed called after me. "Edafe!" he said. "It's time for the noisemaker to leave!" Mohammed hid his emotion but shook my hand and wrapped his arms around me. He held me tightly and whispered some congratulations. I had gone from a scared, alienated outcast, to a coach, a letter writer, a makeshift paralegal—and a friend to many.

I took off my white undershirt and asked all my dorm mates to sign their names on it.

At eight p.m., it was time to count heads. I lay on my concrete bed, and, in the single overhead window, I saw the moon shining brightly. As everyone else participated in the roll call, I waited for the officer to come release me. Though I had no idea what awaited me on the other side of the detention center's walls, I knew I'd rather sleep on the streets of America than spend an extra night in this place.

It had been five months and fourteen days since I was detained at JFK. The only thing I could remember of the outside world in America was the light from a bridge beaming into the back of the bus.

Finally, the officer arrived. "Edafe," he yelled, "pack up your things, let's go." I folded my books and letters into my bedsheet and tied it up like a bag. It was then that Okenna, a fellow Nigerian, hugged me tightly. "Brother," he said. "Pray for me."

I stared into his eye, mustering all the confidence I could. "I got out," I said. "Have faith your day will come too." It was easy to say this, from where I was standing, but this was all I had to offer from my experience. Even if my new friends would make it out of the center, they would first have to survive the dehumanizing process of waiting. As I left, this fact drew into clear focus for me: these centers were designed to derail and detour us, to break us down, to abandon our hope for safety in the United States.

As we left, I stopped at Mohammed's bed to say goodbye, officially. I held my tears as I said, "We will meet in the city upon your release, my friend." He hugged me tightly. Saying goodbye is always hard for me. I could not say goodbye to my family in Nigeria—I hoped I was only saying so long to my new family from the center, and not goodbye.

The rest of my room began to cheer as I walked out, waving. I looked at these men—all striving for what I had. I tried to feel optimistic—I would see some of them on the other side. I knew, though, many deserved my sympathy. Many would never set foot freely in America.

I followed the officer, with my belongings slung over my shoulder. In the hallway, two other men waiting for release that night greeted me. Though, it dawned on me—maybe they weren't waiting for release. Maybe they were to be deported.

We were led to the holding cell—the same place I was kept for twenty-two hours before arriving in Gulf dorm. One way in, and one way out.

An officer asked me, "Do you want to shower?"

"No," I replied. "I am okay." I just wanted to leave.

She asked me to take off my blue jumpsuit and white tennis shoes, and then handed me clothes from the bag I had brought to America. I dressed in clothes from my past life but knew I'd wear them differently here—as a free, gay man.

The doors of the center were opened. "You may go," an officer said.

Outside I was greeted by a vast sky, stars shining brightly above, even against the city lights. I dropped my bags and ran into the road—for a moment I just stood silent and in awe of my freedom.

CHAPTER THREE

Being a New Immigrant in America

"Welcome to America," the border patrol officer had said when I deplaned at JFK. After spending the last five months and fourteen days in a cell, I had come to a different understanding of what those words meant. My welcoming was because I was banished; we could stay in America if we forfeited any affiliation with our homelands. Home became a strange new land, and what we would make of it. This is the task laid before millions of displaced people around the world.

Stories of refugees have dominated the news in America since time immemorial, but we hear less about asylum. "Refugee" is a popular term, but it is quite different from being an asylee. The key difference is political definitions.

My story is not a monolith. It is but one representation of the struggles millions of asylum seekers are faced with. We come from different countries for many different reasons, but most of us strive for opportunities to join a better, more just society. Whether you come in through the border and get detained, or you find yourself in America by other means, we are united in our displacement. Whether due to war, sexual orientation, or natural disaster, one thing remains true: we cannot return home. And yet, it's never that simple. The dream of "coming to America" greets you with no platters of gold.

It wasn't so odd that I found myself again displaced, standing alone in the night, an orphan on the streets of Elizabeth, New Jersey. In truth, I had never had a home of my own. My childhood was met with shuffling from one aunt to another. Even more, while I found shelter with like-minded people in Abuja, I never felt the sense of security and freedom I'd always thought came with feeling at home. My life had been characterized by hardship and resistance, but I always had a place to fall back to at night.

My only sense of security was the piece of paper I clutched in my hand. Indeed, to put it plainly, I was homeless.

Being released in forty-degree weather with no sense of direction made the point incredibly clear: the American incarceration system was efficient in jailing, but not in preparation for an inevitable release. These privately run prisons were designed to create profit off hardship—off the immigrants such as myself seeking protection, only to have our dignity stripped of us, and jailed like criminals. The support I was given was a document with an official stamp. I found myself suddenly ashamed that my new home country would treat immigrants this way.

The moon was waning that night, so I could barely see anything. The creeping noise of crickets and airplanes taking off grew louder as a sudden panic and loneliness set in. I had one focus that evening: survival.

It was then that I remembered First Friends.

Quickly I pulled out the phone I brought with me from Nigeria. It barely turned on, and I had no cell service. I spotted a family walking out of the gate to my right. By the looks of it, they were leaving the ten p.m. visitation. I approached them quickly and was met with stares of contempt. I was a bit uncouth; anyone could describe me perfectly as lacking good manners. Frankly, I was just excited to see people who weren't wearing blue or orange jumpsuits. Perhaps they would take pity on me.

"Hello, I just came out of the detention center," I said, by way of greeting. "I don't have a working phone and I need to make a phone call."

At first, I was met with cautious silence until the young girl among them said, "Sure," and handed me her phone.

On the other end of the line at First Friends, a woman told me to wait in the center's visitation room until someone could pick me up.

"But visitation hours are over," I informed her.

"Wait around," she said. "You'll see a car pull up in the driveway."

I made my way to the waiting room, pretending like I did not see the officer closing up. I sat on top of my bag, my feet shaking, neither relaxed nor comfortable—utterly exhausted. I found my eyes growing heavy.

"Hey," an officer said, jostling me after some time. "We are about to close the visitor's room for the day, you have to leave."

I wanted to explain that I had nowhere to go. Would they perhaps let me spend the night in the center—but no, I was just freed. I couldn't willingly go back inside.

As I pulled myself up, I took my bag and headed for the exit. At the gate, I overheard someone asking after a guy that had been released that night.

When I saw her, she was an elderly white woman whom I approached cautiously. "Hello," she said. "I'm Lorna." She wore a sharp smile and looked at me with fondness. "You should be happy, young man."

"Why?"

"I'm always excited to pick up a newly released friend."

I got into her car. It turns out Lorna was the president of the board of First Friends. But I still didn't know where she was taking me. To her place?

"My place is filled right now," she explained. "My husband and I live close by, and we welcome many new immigrants. We have asylees staying with us." She made a right turn. "Let me drop you at the YMCA." A silence filled the car, but she reassured me, "We'll figure out a solution tomorrow." And with a smile, she added, "I promise."

"Thank you," I said. Finally, some compassion. Some grace. I should have been silently grateful, but I've always been the inquisitive type. "Why did you come this late to pick me up?"

She laughed. "Young man, there's not enough time to explain tonight. I've got to get home to my family. You look like you could use some rest—let's discuss more tomorrow."

At the Y, Lorna chatted familiarly with the receptionist and signed some documents. "Go pick up your bag from the car," she said. "They will take you upstairs."

"Lorna," I said in a whisper. "Will I be safe here?"

She smiled. "Trust me. I have done this more than forty times for different asylees in the last ninety days."

It seemed to me that Lorna and these volunteers were more equipped to help asylees than the government itself.

As Lorna left, I realized I was alone and soon became tense—who would I be sleeping next to? I got to my room, lay on my bed, but could not sleep. Freedom without support was empty and doesn't look like freedom. Sleep was far from my mind that night, despite my exhaustion. But to lie on a bed with a mattress, after months on a concrete slab with a flat bed comparable to sleeping on a floor, was a small bit of paradise.

I hadn't eaten, which contributed to my sleeplessness, so I decided to look for something to eat. My room was among a block filled with families and babies, but I couldn't be certain they weren't as desperate as me. I put my most important documents in my black handbag and took it with me as I wandered off in search of food.

Outside my room was a group of people watching late-night basketball. The receptionist's desk was directly beside the central TV room, with the refrigerator and kitchen on the other side of the desk.

"Good evening," I said to the receptionist. "I am looking for a place to get some food. "Most places are closed now," she replied. "But there's a McDonald's and White Castle nearby."

"Oh," I said, realizing I still didn't have any money. "Okay."

That was when someone tapped me on the back, a big, dark guy with a bald head and a full beard.

"Hey," he said. "Your accent—is it Nigerian?"

"Yes!" I replied.

"My name is Ariside, and I am from Cameroon," he introduced himself. We chatted for a bit, and I learned he was also brought here by First Friends. "I have a friend now. A brother, in fact," he said with a big grin. "Why don't you share my room? We can sort out the paperwork tomorrow."

"I'm looking for something to eat but I don't have any money . . ."

"Come," he said. "I'll make you soup." We walked back to his room and made small talk. What a relief to meet someone from Africa—though we were strangers, our experiences made us quick allies.

He was very polite, welcoming, and friendly; he shared the little he had with me—soap and a towel for the bathroom, his food, his space. He was the guardian angel I needed. It became clear from the smell in his room—a smoky smell covered in scented air freshener, and a mix of other fragrances—that Ariside was addicted to nicotine. But if he had his secrets, so too did I. I surely wasn't about to tell my only new friend about my sexuality. I saw how they treated me in the center at first. Better to be cautious and grateful for now.

But it seemed I would have to figure out what to make of my sexuality now that I was a free man. First, I would rest, wake in the morning, and enjoy a cup of coffee. And then I would call my mother.

* * *

I had not spoken on the phone with my mother in months. The last time she heard from me, she knew I was in Abuja. I wanted to speak with her badly because I myself would be worried if I hadn't heard from my son for a long period of time.

I held the phone, smiling yet nervous. How would I explain the last seven months of my life? She must have heard about the situation in Abuja. I placed the call, watched the call dialing on my screen, each bouncing vibration made it more real that she was on the other side.

She picked up the phone and was silent, because she did not know who was calling her from a foreign number. We both sat on the phone for a few seconds, then I uttered the first words.

"Hi, Mummy," I said, my voice high-pitched, though I did not want her to notice anything different in my voice.

"Edafe!" she howled. "Are you safe? It's been months since anyone has heard from you! Where are you?"

Where to begin? "I am fine," I said, which was mostly true. "I'm in the United States," I said, which was also true.

She sighed, happily, and explained that my old roommate Sylvester had told her I was in jail and asked her to promise not to tell anyone. I believed my old friends in Nigeria would have thought I'd been killed by a mob, or that I'd gone missing like many gay Nigerians. I left my country, telling so few people my plans for safety.

"I'm just so glad you're safe."

"Mummy, how is everyone at home? My brother and sisters?"

"Edafe! They are fine! How are *you*?"

I couldn't say much—I couldn't deliver her the heartache of

knowing how terrible the detention center really was. That was the last thing I wanted.

"I'm okay, I promise."

"Are you sure? You're not just saying that, are you?"

"Mummy, I am fine. I promise. Besides," I said, "America has given me papers to live here."

She could not understand what I was saying. "You have green card now?"

"Not a green card, Mummy. But permission."

She was overjoyed, overprotective of me as she always had been. I started to explain that I had been granted asylum, even though she didn't quite understand what that meant.

"I'm just happy that you're safe," she said softly. "You are alive and well, away from danger. So where are you?"

"Outside of New York City," I said.

"But where are you *living*, Edafe?"

I felt tears well up. How could I tell her I had been imprisoned and was now homeless? I did not want to spoil the joy she felt over my safety. For years I carried the burden—of disappointing her, of causing her hardship over my sexuality. I wanted desperately to make things right—for her and for myself.

I would learn this conversation with my mother was very similar to the conversations that countless new immigrants have with their own parents. How do we navigate our new lives while reestablishing relationships with family back home? I was lucky; many never get to share with their families and friends their stories of displacement. Some families will never know that their loved ones spend nights sleeping in train stations or abandoned buildings, begging for food, all in the name of freedom.

I, too, could not bear to tell my mother I had to beg for food, that I was sleeping at the YMCA, that I didn't know what tomorrow, let alone the future, had in store. All I could say was, "Mummy, none of that matters. I fled to America for one reason: because of who I am."

"Edafe," she said quietly. "People believe you should be punished for being gay."

I did not have the stamina to argue with her about my sexuality. I wanted this to be a celebratory moment.

"I love you, Mum" was all I could muster, and then I told her we would talk again.

Americans themselves may have been kind and sympathetic to a person in my situation, but the American immigration system seemed anything but. Growing up, I watched plenty of American television. I idolized the JabbaWockeeZ, a dance group who won the first season of America's Best Dance Crew; I loved the freedoms of personal style I saw in the American music scene, filled with men and women donning tattoos and piercings all over their faces in glitzy music videos; and I loved *Coming to America*, a film that captured the freedom Americans enjoy. My conservative Nigerian community tended to make fun of Americans. Many Nigerians did not and still do not understand why men would have piercings, wear jewelry, or get tattoos.

Still, it seemed to me that America was the place to be if you wanted to live free of condemnation. When I discovered my sexuality as a teen, the internet was the only place I could find conversations about people like me. The internet gave me glimpses of self-expression, and the freedom to be who I am. America was a choice I made. But I did not imagine I'd struggle with the most basic freedoms: food, clothing, shelter.

I was safe, but things were hardly rosy. I went to churches in Newark to beg for food. I used the internet at the public library to make arrangements for my life after the two weeks at the YMCA. I relied totally on the goodwill of strangers.

Two days after my release, I was using the internet at the Newark public library when Ariside texted me on WhatsApp to tell me the case manager at First Friends, Sally Pillay, was there to pick us up for our social security application appointments. Sally was from South Africa. She came to do her master's in the United States and ended up staying and working with immigrants in New Jersey. I did not have a car, or money to travel, so Sally would drive me to her office, where I could join other asylees who might be applying for social security.

During the ride to Sally's office, she started questioning me. "So, tell me, Edafe, what did you do in Nigeria?"

My first instinct was to lie or be vague—I was still working on being open and honest about myself and my past. Plus, Ariside was in the car. But no, I would have to opt for honesty from here on out, I decided—that was why I was here. "Well," I began. "I worked as an AIDS rights activist and my work was centered around advocating for marginalized people."

She laughed and said, "You have found a home for your work now."

This didn't feel right, though; I had fled Nigeria because of who I was and the work I did. This was a chance for a fresh start. "No," I replied. "Coming to America was an opportunity for me to focus on my life and not work as an activist anymore. It took such a toll."

Sally laughed. "You don't have an option. In Nigeria, you had to speak up to survive." Sally was from South Africa and knew the perils of being a gay person in Africa. She knew, perhaps even before I did, that I couldn't stay quiet any longer.

While we waited for the newly released asylees so we could head to the social security office in Jersey City, we continued to chat with friends on Facebook. Sally went about her day, listening to the voice mails detainees had left for her through the night and early morning. First Friends had an open-door policy, which meant asylees and asylum seekers could walk in at any time and chat with the staff about their cases, ask for support, or sit in to chat with volunteers.

At lunchtime, a volunteer brought a box of pizza, with a big bottle of Sprite. Everyone in the office walked away from their desk and sat at a big table in the computer room. I joined the feast; Rosa, the volunteer coordinator, was in the office that day. Sister Regina was also around, volunteering, even though she was retired. Mrs. Lorna, the board president and a volunteer, was helping out as well.

Ari and I chatted with two folks who were released that day. One from Sudan and the other from Ghana, but they were in a different detention center than my own and had more of a stirring experience. They did not go to court in person, only through video interviews. I wondered how the judge could read their body language. The guy from Sudan explained it was challenging for him because he, the interpreter, and the judges were all remote. Was the interpreter translating correctly? Would this cost him his chance at asylum? I worried about how he would navigate America knowing no English.

We chatted about our different countries and what brought us to America. During the chat, a volunteer asked Sally if she had found someone that would speak on behalf of detainees at the upcoming gala.

Sally replied, "No, not yet. But—I bet Edafe can speak."

Me? Why me? "No," I said. "I don't want to be involved with activism anymore." Sally spent the entire day trying to lure me in. I continually refused, but I began wondering why I was resisting. I could be of help to other people in need. In just two days, First Friends had done so much for me—speaking for them could help the organization in return.

I pondered this as we made our way to the social security office and while we waited in the long line. Sally stayed with us the entire time, just in case we ran into any issues. The application was easy enough, but I was surprised by some of its questions: What country were you born in? When did you enter the United States? What type of visa do you have? What is your current place of residence? At this time, I did not have a place of residence or permanent address, so I used First Friends office address. It was in the car on the way back to the Y that I told Sally I would speak at the gala. "If you can't find anyone else,"

I said. Five days before the gala, I got the call to confirm I was scheduled to speak at the event along with Sally in place of the speaker who could not attend. I was nervous, but it was the least I could do, I decided.

On the night of the gala, I was dressed in my African traditional attire: red hat and multicolored floral print dress. I felt underdressed as soon as we got to the event. Everyone was wearing suits; women wore black dress gowns. I was an outlier in the mix, until Sally arrived—she was in head-to-toe traditional African wear. I smiled upon seeing her.

Sally was very busy at the gala, since she was one of the event's organizers. My seat was preselected to sit with the other speakers at the front of the event, but Sally was nowhere to be found as I waited patiently for my turn to speak.

When it was time for us to speak, Sally was invited to the podium, and she asked me to join her. She spoke about the importance of the work at First Friends and the impact it made in people's lives, pointing to me as an example.

Then I was invited to the mic. The room was filled with over four hundred people. I was afraid to speak about my sexuality and the pain it caused me—but that was why I came to America in the first place. I started off by speaking about how I felt when I arrived in America, how I lost my name to a bed number and an alien number. A First Friend visitor, Lilian, was the first person that called me by my name. She humanized me and gave me a reason to continue the struggle. My experience of fleeing Nigeria, isolation and dehumanization in a detention center, and the importance of a pen pal like Lilian made for a stellar speech that night. When Sally and I stepped off the stage, folks began thanking me for sharing, and implored me to do more work as an immigrants' rights activist.

While I knew this might happen, it did dawn on me that this path might lead to some purpose. The speech's impact on the gala attendees helped me imagine the sort of impact that could come from sharing more of my story.

If the internet was one of the first tools I had in glimpsing the life I wanted in America, it was also one that helped get me on my feet once here. After the gala, at the public library, I connected with a friend, Cristina, through Facebook. Cristina came to Nigeria in 2016 from John Hopkins University to do her PhD dissertation on stigma and its effect on HIV rates among gay men. While she was in Nigeria we bonded, I introduced her around, to help her connect with potential research participants in Abuja, and through this we became friends.

When I chatted with her on Facebook, she told me she had moved from Baltimore to Queens and was working with the department of health. No question asked, she offered me to stay with her rent-free for three months—so long as I wasn't allergic to dogs.

As I packed up what little I had, I said farewell to Ariside and gave him my phone number.

"Let's stay in touch," I offered. I needed a friend here, and so did he. I took the New Jersey PATH train into Manhattan, which deposited me into the belly of Times Square.

My first time in New York City was only in the belly of the Times Square subway station. People buzzed around, trying to make connections in its rusty tunnels, the scent of rodents and sweat wafting about me. I felt breathless to be around so many people in such a tight space. I finally found the 7 train and rode it toward Queens. Cristina was waiting for me at the station to guide me to her apartment, where she had arranged for a blow-up mattress, internet, and occasionally free leftover food from her fridge. What I thought might be a temporary arrangement would last for three months. It's no exaggeration to say she saved my life.

Now to get things off the ground.

I searched on the internet and found a resettlement agency in New York, the International Rescue Committee (IRC) located in Midtown Manhattan. The next morning, I took the 7 train from my friend Cristina's place in Sunnyside, Queens, back to Times Square. I was wearing khaki shorts and a too-big winter coat I had gotten at the YMCA, which swallowed me up because I was skinny from months in the detention center.

The agency appointed me a case manager, Jessica, a blond, blue-eyed, tall lady. She registered me in the system, explained the benefits program, which offered me two hundred dollars for two months to pay for things like transportation. My first task was to get a job. If I got a job by the end of the second month and kept it for three months, with proof of my pay stubs, I would be given another two hundred dollars. Jessica handed me over to the employment officer, who was tasked with prepping my résumé and helping me find a job. But the jobs the officer showed me were all entry-level service gigs: washing dishes in kitchens, cleaning beds in hotels, arranging stuff in warehouses. I assumed because I had a college degree from Nigeria, I'd be qualified for something a bit loftier.

Four weeks of sleeping in Cristina's living room went by and still I had no job. I knew I had to care for myself or run the risk of becoming a burden on her generosity. So again, I tried an employment agency, this time in Queens.

I began early on a Thursday morning to make my first visit to the employment agency and dressed as though I was meeting the CEO of a multimillion-dollar company. First impressions matter—especially for people in my circumstances. I brought two copies of my résumé, my social security card, and an I-94 card showing my documented asylee status. I waited outside with two other people before the doors opened at eight a.m. I quickly realized no one was dressed as nicely as I was.

The reception area was quite big and filled with posters in languages of all kinds, from Spanish to Chinese. I was a bit surprised, because I thought most things in America would only be written in English. I tried to compose myself and quell my nerves—my tapping leg—until an agent called me to her desk.

She sat in her chair, wearing a light purple dress. "What sort of skills do you have, Mr. Okporo?" she asked. She seemed interested and spoke quickly, as though she might hire me in the next five minutes.

I started speaking professional jargon—about my experiences in key populations, a term we use in HIV work to categorize high-risk behavior such as sex workers and drug users. I told her about my degree in nutrition, thinking it would appeal to employers.

She smiled. "You need to lower your expectations," she said. "You cannot get most jobs without a professional license." She explained I might be better off starting with something like dishwashing.

"No, no," I protested.

"Well," she said, "what else might you be suited for? What about working at a hotel . . . ?"

"No," I said. I was new to the system, and I believed I could get a job as a nutritionist or as a program officer. Perhaps I was being unrealistic, expecting more, but I did not believe I had come to America only to work as someone's cleaner.

"Here," she finally said, writing down an address on a piece of paper and sliding it to me across the desk. "Show up here tomorrow. It's a frozen-food processor—they're looking for an account officer."

With great optimism, I woke up early the next day, showered, and walked Cristina's dog, Harley. By the time Cristina woke, I told her I would be going to my first day at my new job.

She smiled. "I hope you know you can stay here as long as you need to," she said.

"No," I said. "I just want to be able to take care of myself."

The address I was given was not far from Cristina's apartment, so I decided to walk under the industrial bridges of Long Island City into Greenpoint. I wore heavy pants—even though it was summer—with a tucked-in long-sleeve shirt, no tie. I wanted to be formal and casual at once—though I wasn't in Africa, it was still a hot day in June. The address led me to a warehouse with two delivery trucks in front. The men were busy off-loading the trucks as I approached and asked for the person whose name I'd been given.

"Oh," one of the guys said. "That's the manager. He'll be in soon." I waited in reception, where someone spoke in a foreign language—Japanese? Korean?—and the odor of fish and fresh produce overtook the smell of the cologne I was wearing. Gradually, as I noticed what people were wearing, I realized I might be overdressed for the occasion again.

When the manager arrived—a short, well-dressed man just over five feet tall—he asked if I knew what I'd be doing.

"No," I replied, "but I know I will be working as an account officer."

He chuckled lightly with a brush of a smile on his face. "Yes, you are an account officer. That means you will be in charge of counting the produce that arrives in the cold room for storage."

I felt heartbroken; this was not at all what I expected. "Forgive me, sir," I said. "But I don't think I can do this job." I wasn't expecting much for my first job in America, but I expected more than this. I called the employment agency, asking for a full refund, which they could give me, but not for twenty-one days.

I called the refugee resettlement agency and my case manager. Certainly, she'd understand my frustration.

"Edafe," she said. "Yes, it's a job!" I've learned over time that resettlement agencies force refugees into doing entry-level jobs despite their qualifications from their home countries—they do this in order to check a box, to call us "successfully resettled." To them, work is work. What they fail to take into account is our mental health—the trauma we've suffered through seeking protection in America, only to find ourselves underutilized in the workforce. It was a tough realization.

I walked back to the apartment, thinking of what else I would do. I explained the situation to Cristina, and she told me about job board websites where I might find better luck. I began going through the sites and applied to as many as I could in a single day.

On Craigslist, I saw that a not-for-profit organization was looking for street canvassers, to show up at their office downtown. It was a referral post—if you showed up, you got a job on the spot. The draw for me was that this group was canvassing to raise money for LGBTQ organizations.

Though I kept trying to run from my activism, and the ghosts of its past, I still needed a job.

I got to their office early the next morning and was quickly put into an orientation group, where I was paired with a group leader. They would work in the morning, and I would observe; in the afternoon, I would try my hand at canvassing on my own.

We were on the streets near Battery Park under the hot sun, just a few steps from the Staten Island Ferry, the Statue of Liberty visible in the distant waters. We'd hail passersby, asking them to sign up in support of progressive campaigns to protect LGBTQ rights. I quickly saw that it was hard, dispiriting work, begging strangers to donate to a cause—one that was so close to my own struggle—only to be met with rudeness, or worse, no response at all. But this was my first induction into the gay rights activism in America.

In the summer of 2017, I got my first paycheck: eighty-seven dollars. It was very heartwarming to see my name on a pay stub. But I knew the job would not be sustainable in the long run. I saw the shoes of my coworkers, completely worn out.

Most mornings after canvassing, I would rest and continue my job search. By now, I'd grown used to the American coffee at Starbucks, where I'd post up and borrow their free Wi-Fi and air-conditioning. It became my makeshift office—where I'd read emails, send out my résumé, and watch YouTube videos on interview preparation.

One afternoon, I received a call from my case manager—a catering company called Eat Offbeat was looking for a kitchen manager. "You have a degree in food science," she reminded me. They could meet me in forty-five minutes. I ran through Sunnyside like a madman, back to Cristina's apartment, where I brushed my teeth and scrubbed my face and armpits with a bit of water. I couldn't afford an Uber, so I ran to the 7 train—by the time I was cooling off under the air-conditioning, I realized I wasn't wearing a belt.

"I didn't expect you to be so well dressed," Manal Kahi, Eat Offbeat's CEO, said with a smile. She needed someone big enough to lift boxes and do inventory. This job was not way different from the job I was offered by the employment agency, but I saw an opportunity to grow. Eat Offbeat was a startup organization with heart behind it—Manal was an immigrant herself, and the business model was built around helping refugees. The kitchen was out in Long Island City, just walking distance from Cristina's apartment.

"Can you start right away?" she asked.

The first social media post I made from America was on Facebook. It was a picture of me at Newark Penn Station with the United States flag behind me. I am gay and I am proud of who I am, I wrote. People who hate me do so only because they don't have the courage to be themselves.

I wanted to celebrate my newfound freedom, but it was a complete mistake. Hateful messages immediately rolled in. People said terrible things about me—about my mother, for carrying me for nine months only to bring a gay child into the world. While I wanted to share my new life—my joy in safety—it was clear no one was celebrating along with me. I deleted Facebook and all social media platforms from my phone. I found myself not wanting to have anything to do with Nigerians. I just wanted to focus on my life here in America.

Homophobia travels across every border in the world. It's hard for many people to understand gay people—when they think of us, they see us solely as sexual beings and nothing else. To them, we are not people who deserve love and compassion. Nigerians in America, too, did not see me as part of their community—I was a homosexual first, and wholly.

Gay asylum seekers who migrate to America constantly face this dilemma. Our diaspora communities shun us for being too sparkly or chastise us for adopting the Western ways of doing things. I could change—it might be a phase, or perhaps if I was isolated enough, I'd see I was wrong. But I came to America to be myself, not to be drawn into another closet.

The Nigerian community in America shunned me, and the U.S. gay community certainly did not welcome me with open arms. The gay community was supposed to be my home, my fortress, but it was much more difficult to access as a Black gay immigrant.

You have to have a certain level of class to join the gays. They welcome those who look good to mingle with in public. Online,

I searched for a gay community—if not for romance, then at least for friendship—but many people had no understanding of what I'd been through. They wanted to have fun; they liked your accent, but they didn't know or care about you not having a place to lay your head at night.

I did have some friends, at the very least—people like Sylvester, whom I had met in Abuja, and was now also a gay Nigerian man living in America. I remember one night asking him to go to a gay club, but he refused and told me to go on my own if I wanted to.

"Why?" I asked. We used to go out to clubs together in Abuja, and now we were free in America.

"You are free," he said. "I am not." Sylvester was still waiting for his status to be granted; Sylvester was what we call an affirmative asylum seeker, whereas I went through the defensive asylum process. He did not declare asylum at the border, which is why he did not get detained like me. He attended church with many Nigerians in New York. He couldn't risk them finding out about him being gay—what if he wasn't granted asylum? He'd be returned to Nigeria to face persecution.

Though I often felt dissatisfied and disappointed by my inability to find a community in America that fully accepted and celebrated who I was, my life was taking shape in other ways. I had a steady job at the catering company, where I'd now been employed for about five months. I finally saved enough to move out of Cristina's apartment, but not enough to live in New York City. So I moved to Jersey City to save money, commuting by train with all of the other commuters. I felt like I was finally on my feet, but I had no one to share it with. My first year of living in America was isolating; I constantly felt misunderstood.

I also quickly realized I had inherited the oppression that comes with having dark skin and an accent. The biases toward me for having an accent are probably stronger than being a non-white in America. When you meet someone, the first visible difference is your skin color; the next is how you speak. *Where are you from?* is usually their first probing question. Being from Africa comes with baggage to explain—it is a large continent with vastly different social and cultural norms, languages, and lifestyles that vary from country to country.

I often felt heartbroken, thinking of my family and the home I'd left behind. I had a job and an apartment, but I wasn't exactly a full-fledged member of society. Then, I didn't feel othered because of my sexual orientation, but because of my refugee status. If I couldn't find what I was looking for in New York, at least I had the freedom to try looking somewhere else. But I felt something strongly about New York. Gay people holding hands on the sidewalk, carting their kids around in strollers, kissing on the subway. Would I find that somewhere else? It was hard to know, and though I wanted to build a life in this city, the reality was that I could hardly afford to. New York's cost of living is expensive for most people, let alone a new immigrant. After three months, I had no choice but to move somewhere more affordable: New Jersey, the place I had fled with bright eyes.

The first few weeks of commuting from New Jersey was fun. I read on the subway, listened to podcasts, and pretended to be among the bankers commuting into Manhattan, returning at night, exhausted from a laborious workday. After a month, the commute to and from the city began to wear on me, so I finally decided to quit my job and focus my life in Jersey. I could kill two birds with one stone, find a job in Jersey City and continue to be on the board of First Friends.

I found a job in Paterson, New Jersey, working with the Hyacinth AIDS Foundation. I took this as an opportunity to start anew, and to reconnect with the work I had been trying to flee yet found myself returning to again and again. With Hyacinth, I was doing the kind of work I had done in Abuja: supporting LGBTQ community members trying to access HIV treatment.

Still, I could not afford a car—which meant lengthy journeys by bus and train with early mornings and late nights. Worse yet, while the gay community of New York was unwelcoming, the gay community of New Jersey seemed almost nonexistent. Generic whiteness superseded any sense of community. When I visited one of the only gay bars in downtown Jersey City, I sat alone and watched people laugh and dance together. At twenty-seven, I felt alone more than ever. Life was hard in Nigeria as a gay man. Running away was harder. It seemed everyone was afraid of me. During my first Gay Pride month in America, I spent the celebratory weekend alone in my apartment watching people on TV embrace themselves. I may have been out, but I was still too afraid to go to an event, with thoughts of my past traumas haunting my mind. I was numb, and even contemplated suicide.

I came to the United States with faith for a better tomorrow. Arriving in this country, getting my asylum, were signs of a promising tomorrow. It would take time, but I would rise from these ashes. I knew my community back home in Nigeria would be disappointed that I made it to America only to take my own life. I had to persist—for me, for Bobby and Emmanuel, to have our stories told.

I tried burying myself in my work helping gay, bisexual, and transgender youths access information and resources about HIV/AIDS, but it wasn't as fulfilling as I'd hoped. HIV/AIDS was not an epidemic in America as it was in Abuja—people here, unlike my friends back home, were not dying from this disease in the same volume. At my loneliest, I turned to the one place I felt some sense of belonging: First Friends of New Jersey. I advocated for immigrants locked up in the detention center I'd been in not long ago. This felt like a return home, to something familiar. In June of 2017, I was nominated to the board of First Friends; I joined the board and an opportunity to work with Sally again.

Though I had run away from activism, this much was clear: activism had been my friend for a long time, and it was my friend again. So was Sally—we began wider community outreach to educate people about the asylum process and the terrors of the detention centers. The volunteers, who would go to centers and work with us, made the same observation again and again: asylum seekers were *afraid* of being released, because they would have nowhere to live. Better to stay locked up with a concrete slab to sleep on and be fed daily than to be homeless. I knew that feeling, and I knew that dissonance—the America I had always known as a child to be the so-called paradise, was not. But gears were beginning to turn in my head—perhaps I could help find a solution to that problem.

One evening, Sally took me to a speaking event in Bayonne, New Jersey. After hearing me speak that evening, I met a lady named Emily and her husband, who were both interested in learning more about immigration detention centers. Emily would become a steadfast visitor to people in detention centers in the months to come. It finally clicked for me: my voice had real power. I had to keep speaking up. I found myself attending meetings of activist groups in New York; hearing their passion, and their vision for change, left me feeling energized and compelled to act as I sat on the PATH train back to New Jersey.

I had no option other than to act. I had to leave New Jersey and return to New York in order to support the immigrant community, to organize rallies and protest, and be involved where people were hurting the most. I had told Sally of my disinterest in working with access to health care services in New Jersey because it was not as fulfilling as I had hoped. The plight of migrants was more urgent for me. I met people like Aliyu, who told me of his experience. He was released at ten p.m. from the Essex County detention center and had no contact with an organization like First Friends, so he had to sleep on the street. He was found the next day by a First Friends volunteer who was going to visit a detainee at the center, and who brought him to a shelter in Newark. He attended First Friends volunteer training and shared his story; I was traumatized to hear the story of another asylum seeker who had a similar experience to mine. I told Sally to be on the lookout for me if a position opened up in the immigrant space; I wanted to be informed.

In the spring of 2018, I was on a train from Paterson when I received an email from Sally. Marianne Scharf, the current director of a shelter called RDJ was planning to leave.

RDJ was a homeless shelter in Harlem, New York, named after a homelessness advocate, Robert Daniel Jones. I was afraid to apply, due to the uncertain salary. It would also mean leaving my first real job with health insurance, a 401(k), and vacation benefits, to basically take on a job that I was not sure I would have in nine to twelve months. Still, I knew I could do so much good there.

I arrived for my interview at the shelter's church, dressed in nice pants and a long-sleeve shirt (I'd learned the best way to dress for these jobs by now). At the first sight of a church, I was apprehensive. The director, Marianne, welcomed me and explained there was no office in the shelter, so we'd have to chat in the church. The reverend of the parish joined the meeting, and they both questioned me about my experience and why I wanted to take the job with no guarantee the position would be funded beyond nine months.

To be honest, that didn't bother me as much as their affiliation with the church. That was until I met the rector, Reverend Mary, who happened to be a lesbian married to an African American woman, with two children of their own. Still, the pay was very little for the responsibility I would be taking on—I would be fundraising, managing communications, case management, and, of course, running the shelter. But when they offered me the job—reminding me they were doing so because of my background, my passion, and my own experiences as a refugee—it made perfect sense.

And so, I moved back. Rinse and repeat. I did not have a place to stay and was back on Cristina's couch. The commute from Sunnyside to Harlem wasn't easy though, and I began wondering if perhaps living with Sylvester might be a better option for housing. We were roommates in Abuja, after all.

I tried contacting Sylvester when I returned to New York, and after some hesitation, he finally agreed for us to meet downtown at a pizzeria close to the Oculus, the former site of the World Trade towers. We'd known each other long enough that I knew something was off when he walked into the pizzeria. He was timid and not the least bit excited to see his longtime friend.

"Hey, Sylvester," I said, welcoming him to our table. "Everything okay?"

He looked worried, trying to get the conversation over and done with. "Edafe, do you think we could actually catch up another time?"

I was stunned. This was our first time seeing each other since he'd left Nigeria in March 2016. I refused and told him he had to stay for just a little while. We caught up, compared notes on our immigration cases. Unlike him, at this point I had been granted asylum, so I wasn't sure if it was this—jealousy?—or something else that made him abruptly stand after half an hour.

"I really should get going," he said. I was so happy to see him; why we would leave so soon?

It was then that the manager came out of the kitchen, with a smoky face and a black apron. He met Sylvester's eyes, and then looked at his wristwatch. As it turned out, Sylvester worked at this pizzeria as a dishwasher. He was ashamed to tell me, I realized—this friend who gave me a home in Abuja after leaving Bobby's place. He explained that his asylum application had continued to be delayed, so he took to working in the kitchen to make money and pay his rent. In Nigeria, Sylvester worked as a sales representative for Glenfiddich, had a college degree, and had traveled abroad. In New York, he was working illegally because he did not have working papers due to his stalled asylum process.

"You got here after me, and you're doing well," he explained. He was tired and exhausted by the asylum process being delayed again and again. My presence only made it worse.

"I should return to the kitchen," he said. I hugged him tightly, hoping to convey to him through my embrace that he had nothing to be ashamed of. I had been in his very shoes not long ago. "All will be well," I whispered. He pushed me away softly. But then he gripped my arm, and with bulging eyes he said, "I am happy for you."

Sylvester had a place to lay his head at night, but he was clearly uncertain about his future. He kept a low profile and saved every dime he earned, fearing that at any moment he might be asked to leave America. Better to not be financially unprepared for that reality.

Asylum seekers are the brutalized masses yearning for freedom. Among the different immigration categories such as H-1B visas, diversity visa (known as the U.S. lottery), and others, asylum seekers are offered the fewest protections, and have seen very little fundamental change to the asylum process over decades, despite constant changes to the asylum legislation itself. Just like in February 2018, then U.S. Attorney General Jeff Sessions signed a new asylum law known as Last In, First Out—which made cases for those arriving after this date easier to pursue. Those folks would have to have their cases reviewed within twenty-one days of arriving. This may sound like an advantage, to expedite the process, but it was intentionally punitive—it largely fast tracked the deportations for those who were denied protection.

Additionally, it made cases like Sylvester's harder to pursue, as it caused perpetual delays for hearings. Those arriving before February 2018 were essentially stuck in limbo.

Many new asylum seekers who arrived after 2018 received protection within two to three months of their application, which has now created an extensive backlog for asylum seekers like Sylvester. At the time of this writing, Sylvester has yet to receive a call for an asylum interview, despite applying in 2016. People like Sylvester cannot leave the country, let alone the state they reside in, because looking for work in other states could jeopardize their application within their state of residence, creating uncertain futures.

What are we left with, if the legislative process seems to actively work against those seeking protection? Often, it's goodwill. Think of my friend Cristina; think of the pro bono legal representation I received in the detention center. These situations are not so uncommon. With no centralized system in place to care for those seeking protection, we are often left turning to nonprofit organizations; shelters, church basements, single-room apartments, and train cars often become our homes.

In recent years, the Trump administration aggressively attacked not only the legal process of asylum, but the rhetoric of the issue as well. Under Trump, the abiding line had been that America is full. People should wait in line for their chance to emigrate here. But this is hardly a new phenomenon. If immigration has been the hallmark of American progress, then policing immigration laws has been the impediment to its evolution. Nearly all U.S. presidents since 1980 have increased the amount of people detained each day in America.* The use of detention centers was not unique to the Trump administration—this had been an American policy, an ethos to prevent and deter Black and brown people from coming into this country, for years. The Reagan administration notably declared the War on Drugs. The people who suffered most from these wars were Cuban and Haitian immigrants who got locked up in detention centers. Internal memos from the Reagan administration cited the use of detention centers as a means of deterring Black immigrants from coming into the country.†

But if we look farther back, we see America has outsourced cheap labor in the form of migrant workers for decades, even before World War II. But during World War II, America failed to let in refugees, leaving millions to die. As a country, we said, "never again" and co-signed the refugee act of 1951. In 1952, the United Nations came together to sign the agreement to protect people whose countries were not willing or able to protect them. This caused a surge of refugee resettlement in America—a time when America was seen as a beacon of hope for those fleeing persecution due to war, violence, and discrimination. President Clinton signed the 1994 Crime Bill into law—which led to heavy policing of Black communities and the subsequent mass incarceration of Black immigrants—and also made it legal to expunge

* Emily Kassie, "Detained: How the United States Created the Largest Immigrant Detention System in the World," The Marshall Project, September 24, 2019, https://www.themarshallproject.org/2019/09/24/detained.

† Smita Ghosh, "How Migrant Detention Became American Policy," *Washington Post*, July 19, 2019, https://www.washingtonpost.com/outlook/2019/07/19/how-migrant-detention-became-american-policy/.

illegal immigrants with minor offenses. Of course, after 9/11, the formation of ICE under George W. Bush created eight units to protect our borders but has since grown to include more than 128 units focused on terrorizing immigrants and communities of color.

There has been incremental progress. In enacting the Immigration and Nationality Act (INA) of 1965, Congress eliminated the quota system based on national origin for immigrants seeking refuge; their intent was to equalize immigration opportunities for groups previously subjected to discriminatory immigration laws and practices. The Refugee Act of 1980 signed by President Jimmy Carter was a new lift in American migration policy. This was the first comprehensive amendment of U.S. general immigration laws designed to face the realities of modern refugees by stating a clear-cut national policy to accept people fleeing persecution on humanitarian grounds and providing a flexible mechanism to meet the rapidly shifting developments of the world.

In recent years, the use of immigration detention and fast-track deportation started under the Clinton administration's 1994 Crime Bill, and followed in 2005 when George W. Bush launched Operation Streamline along the Texas border. The policy adopted a zero-tolerance approach to border crossings and called for the criminal prosecution of all migrants who crossed the border illegally. It also led to the separation of families and locking up a vast number of immigrants in detention. In 2014, during the Obama era, we saw the declaration of the child migrant crisis and the use of military bases to house the flood of unaccompanied minors to the border, which became the model for what morphed into an extreme response by the Trump administration of putting adults, mothers, and children in blankets behind bars.

President Barack Obama was labeled the "Deporter-in-Chief" by the migrants from Central America whom I met in the detention center. Despite the high number of deportations under his administration, the U.S. did see an increase in the number of refugees permitted entry to America. The Obama administration also expanded the eligibility for asylum to include people fleeing violence in Central America. Some immigration activists call the Obama administration wicked because of the increase in deportation; the focus of the deportations, however, remained on people who had committed violent crimes and those considered a threat to the well-being of Americans.

The use of detention centers was prevalent under the Obama administration, but the treatment of migrants in detention centers was different. The goal was to use the buildings as a processing center for migrants either to be held and processed into the country or deported back to their home countries. The intention was right, but the system remained oppressive. And Obama's signature DACA provision, a pathway for immigrants brought to this country as children, does not negate the fact that his administration used a system of oppression against immigrants that set the stage for an extreme opposing reaction to sensible immigration policies.

When discussing former president Donald Trump's migrant policies, we must not argue in support or opposition to him as a president, but instead focus on an argument of humanity. Under his leadership, we saw some of the most dramatic changes in our nation's history of immigration policies. Trump favored the use of detention centers by private owners, which resulted in a spike in the stock prices of companies that ran private prisons, like the GEO Group. The GEO Group stock price was $13.36 when Donald Trump won the Republican Party nomination in August of 2016; when I left the New Jersey detention center in April 2017, their stock price had more than doubled to $33.32.*

Today, the American detention center system is the largest in the world. More than fifty-four thousand people are detained each day in America, in all fifty states. Again, the volume of detained migrants is directly related to the for-profit prison systems that America, and the Trump administration, favored—this system is in place to exploit immigrants, rather than to protect them.

Since my arrival to this country in 2016, immigration has resurfaced again and again as a hot-button issue in the American social psyche. This was particularly true in 2016—an election year—as it was most noticeably used as a talking point by then presidential hopeful Donald Trump. Trump unilaterally described immigrants as "illegal"—criminals and destitutes bent on stripping Americans of their resources and jobs. When I arrived here, I had no idea who Donald Trump was; his administration didn't know me, but they claimed to. I can say with confidence that Trump attempted to undo progressivism within U.S. immigration policy, leaving America with a reputation for being heartless toward immigrants.

Under Trump, our country welcomed the lowest number of refugees in modern American history. This is of course linked to his administration's policies such as the war on immigrant families. Trump ruthlessly attempted to remove immigrants who had

* https://finance.yahoo.com/quote/GEO?.tsrc=applewf.

well-established ties to this country, and who had no criminal records. He famously labeled migrants from Africa as coming from "shithole countries,"* further linking his policy agenda to divisive rhetoric that immigrants came in two classes—desirable and undesirable. He signed an executive order to build a wall at the U.S.-Mexico border and declared a national emergency to fund its construction. We witnessed various cruel changes in immigration policy, such as separating mothers and children when detained at the border. We almost saw an end to DACA. And, after only seven days in office, he instituted a Muslim ban, preventing immigrants from Muslim-majority countries from entering the United States under the guise of "protecting us against foreign terrorists." Of course, the plan was really to limit migration to America in a manner that clearly echoed the Reagan administration's attitudes toward Cuban and Haitian migrants.

The Trump administration's exclusionary policies did not stop at discrimination based on skin tone or country of origin. On June 15, 2020, the Trump administration and the Department of Justice proposed a new set of asylum regulations. This 161-page document was filled with regulations that would limit people seeking asylum based on sexual orientation and gender identity. Overall, 4.3 percent of U.S. adults identify as lesbian, gay, bisexual, or transgender, according to Gallup's latest estimate from its June 2016 to June 2017 tracking data. That is up from

* Ali Vitali, Kasie Hunt, and Frank Thorp V, "Trump Referred to Haiti and African Nations as 'Shithole' Countries," NBC News. January 11, 2018, https://www.nbcnews.com/politics/white-house/trump-referred-haiti-african-countries-shithole-nations-n836946.

3.9 percent a year ago and 3.4 percent in Gallup's initial estimate in 2012.* Statistically, that would indicate about 4 percent of the 70 million people displaced globally might be LGBTQ, which leaves 2.8 million migrants fleeing persecution based on sexual orientation and gender identity without a safe refuge in America. If you recall Nigeria's oppressive anti-LGBTQ laws, it remains not only unsafe but also illegal to be gay in many parts of the world.

Along with LGBTQ discrimination, the tactics were threefold. First, the Trump administration favored denying due process for asylees, deferring to border patrol agents to determine if one's fear of persecution was credible. Based on these assessments and a general sense that our immigration system has been historically overloaded, many were denied their fair day in court. Had I arrived when these policies were in place, it's very likely that I would have been deported back to Nigeria—the country where I was nearly beaten to death because of my sexual orientation. Second, these new regulations barred refugees from seeking protection if you had visited more than two countries prior to arriving in the United States. For example, if you fled from Uganda and the cheapest flight would have at least two stops before landing in America, this new regulation would have prohibited you from seeking asylum. This is totally an unimaginable scenario for asylees who arrive in America by way of these other countries due to transit rather than hoping to go through their immigration processes. Third, the definition of

* Jeffrey M. Jones, "In U.S., 102% of LGBT Adults Now Married to Same-Sex Spuse," Gallup, June 22, 2017, https://news.gallup.com/poll/212702/lgbt-adults-married-sex-spouse.aspx?g_source=Social+Issues&g_medium=newsf.

"firm resettlement" in another country was changed under these new regulations to encompass staying for more than a few hours in a country otherwise deemed "safe." This meant that even a long layover in a country like Germany or the Netherlands would render you ineligible for asylum in the U.S.

The history of America's immigration system is complicated. But now, at a time where authoritarian governments are on the rise, we have seen swift action from the previous administration to close our borders to people who see America as their last best hope for freedom.

The social and political climate toward displaced people during the Trump era was *the* polarizing political issue of our times—under Trump, refugees and asylees were painted as our enemies, no matter how much of his rhetoric was dangerously ignorant and largely based on unfounded conspiracies. During the final presidential debate of 2020, former vice president Joe Biden claimed that Donald Trump was the only president that wanted asylum seekers to seek U.S. asylum while waiting outside of America.* True, the Trump administration had shaken up the asylum system drastically, and clearly they had a fundamental misunderstanding of what asylum means. Asylum is a form of protection you seek when you get to the border of a country; under Trump, the definition was not only diluted but misunderstood. Asylum seekers coming to our border to seek protection *are* doing it "the right way." This is, by definition, the process

* "Debate transcript: Trump, Biden final presidential debate moderated by Kristen Welker," *USA Today*, October 23, 2020, https://www.usatoday.com/story/news/politics/elections/2020/10/23/debate-transcript-trump-biden-final-presidential-debate-nashville/3740152001/.

deemed "correct" by international mandates. Under Trump, the abiding opinion was that America is full. If you want to come here, do it the right way. If not, try somewhere else.

By all accounts, I "did it the right way." These people coming to our border to seek asylum, according to the 1980 Refugee Act, are doing it the right way. Under Trump, "doing it the right way" was also the convenient scapegoat for the administration to deter immigration. This gave birth to one of our most hideous immigration policies: the REMAIN in Mexico Act for asylum seekers. This policy has given way to the victimization of hundreds of asylum seekers. There are reports of people being raped in camps in Mexico, robbed, and most migrants missing their court dates because they don't have an address in Mexico where their court papers can be sent. It's sometimes hard to process why the Trump administration turned their back on immigrants from Latin America and Third World countries. Perhaps there's no better explanation than his own declaration of those countries being "shitholes."

While the president had a proverbial megaphone with which to proclaim all immigrants were criminals, terrorists, or both, the underlying fact remains: the United States is not full. The only line of migrants at our borders are housed inside detention centers, sleeping on concrete slabs.

We have come to call the United States of America a home for strangers. This is who we claim to be, a nation of immigrants. This is why Americans have been proud to call this country the land of the free and the home of the brave. America, to those of us on the outside, has always been the place where anyone is welcome—you can come here with nothing, to become something, someone.

Indeed, holding strong opinions on a process you have never experienced is the epitome of ignorance. During the Trump era—in matters of immigration and all others—believing and upholding baseless conspiracies became the norm. Many have been quick to pass judgment about *who* has fled for America, without thinking much about *why* and from *where* they fled. I've always believed that in America, we aren't meant to judge people for who they are when they arrived, but for who they can become by living here.

Asylum seekers tend to seek one thing: to live our truest lives, free of persecution and hatred, in a new home. In the wake of the Trump presidency, life here has become more or less a battle to justify our daily existence, as much as we strive to be who we thought we would become upon arrival. America promises liberty and justice for all, but we must ask ourselves: What is the America we dream of for ourselves—and what good comes from preventing others from accessing that freedom? Who gets to enjoy freedom? We "foreigners" are continually asked if when we pledge our allegiance, is it to America? I don't consider myself anti-America for asking America to uphold her promise.

I am lucky to have been granted protection. I am thankful for my pathway to citizenship. But there is a lot more to be done. Immigration in America should not be viewed as a quid-pro-quo situation: you give me protection; I seal my mouth forever. When I question America, I do so with optimism of what we could become if we care for the displaced. I do so for myself, and for the people I know, like Sylvester, and the people I do not yet know. Asylees are not handed their freedom on a gold platter. Most immigrants I know are especially hardworking, dedicated, and gracious people. This is why we succeed. This is why we persevere. This shared experience is why we continue to fight to be a part of American society—one that is just, for all.

While I wouldn't learn more about the detention and immigration process until many months after I had been released, it's important to understand the ways in which my experience was so normal—that the system itself was designed to keep a bottleneck effect in place to prevent migrants from coming into America.

We cannot discuss anti-immigrant narratives without looking back to the formation of modern-day immigration policies in America. This conversation dates back to the perception of non-Blacks and Indigenous people being viewed as non-Americans. I recall a quote that said humans are not shaped by carbons but by stories, and the stories we've told ourselves in the First World is one of superiority. We are superior not only to other species of animals; our superiority spans other humans living in Third World countries. The American system has always been based on excluding people.

The orientation process for new immigrants is nonexistent, which is core to the issue. When you arrive in a country as big as the United States, there is no federal directory, no bulletin on what to do, where to access housing, shelter, or legal support. This would not cost the government much to reform the welcoming process for asylum seekers, to make it a more compassionate and humane system.

The main conversation goes back to why the law is so easily changed to affect the most marginalized. Asylum seekers are at the mercy of these policies, including those already living in

America. ICE raids in communities to extract people living in America disproportionately target Black and brown people, as we happen to be easy targets for law enforcement. The loopholes in the system are created by the autonomy granted to the executive branch to change U.S immigration laws at will, which makes immigration a topic of discussion year after year. And yet, we still have no concrete solutions for improving the system and ensuring oversight. I believe the solution to U.S immigration is a reform of our immigration process.

The need for reform of U.S immigration policies is deeply seated in the inhumane treatment of people seeking protection in America. After making the long journey to the United States, you are met with a complex system that is meant to punish and deter. I have seen this firsthand when I was detained by immigration, and through my work as the director of the RDJ Refugee Shelter.

Not-for-profit organizations are doing great work in terms of offering resources to new immigrants, but they don't have the resources or capacity to provide housing or structure. We need to center housing, specifically, in our reforms to asylum laws and practices in America. I believe the federal government housing program has to be extended to provide accommodation for displaced people seeking refuge in America. Imagine all we could do just by diverting the money going to maintain the private prisons and centers detaining refugees into actually helping people, arming them with information and resources. Imagine how different my early days in this country could have looked.

CHAPTER FOUR

Being a Black Gay Man in America

I remember when I saw a white person for the first time.

It is unacceptable to grow up in Warri and be claustrophobic. Waffairians are known for not minding our own business. In fact, we lived in each other's businesses. The compound I grew up in was popularly known as the "I better pass my neighbor" structure. These buildings were large, connected houses, with more than fourteen rooms and each individual family occupying a single room. Because my father moved into the compound at a young age and was close with the landlord, he was able to secure one of the bedrooms in the front of the building—this meant we had more space, yet we all shared the two communal bathrooms and two communal toilets located in the backyard of the compound. To the side of our structure was a shared hanging line for all fourteen families to dry their clothes, which was a point of contention—each family had a day for washing their clothes, and hanging your wet clothes on the line on the wrong day would end in a fight.

We would fetch our drinking water from the mud well dug in the front of the compound—the compound immediately in front of ours had their toilets located close to our drinking water. If they had a leak, it was often disastrous. Were a stranger to walk into our neighborhood, they might think we were a big family living together—but the compounds themselves were traditionally made up of many strangers, all speaking different languages and bringing their unique cultures to the shared space. I remember in the late nineties when my compound was approved to be among the first places to get a borehole for clean drinking water; we celebrated.

Our landlord's family lived in a single-family home close to the big house. One of their sons was living abroad in London, but the year I turned nine, he was due to return—as part of the Nigerian tradition, it is customary for a son to introduce his wife to his family for a blessing before the church wedding. Details trickled in through gossip—most notably, that his bride was an *Oyibo* (white) woman. People have said it was the wife's connections that made us among the first people to get the drilled borehole in our compound. We heard the wedding was slated for a Sunday evening, to take place in our landlord's living room. As an elder, my dad was invited to sit in the living room—a seat of great honor, to pay respect—while my mum would be would among the women to dress the bride in our traditional attire.

Marriage is a big deal in our culture. Not only are there customs for a big celebration with plenty of food and music, but everyone also looked forward to getting, as we called it, "the bride price." This is something like a dowry—when a woman was given away in marriage, the husband would often pay her family.

We could tell how well-off a family was by the bride price—if you killed a cow, you were wealthy; a chicken or a goat, not so much. It was widely known that getting married to an *Oyibo* woman meant their family had money to spend.

The day of the ceremony, our compound was clearly the center of the universe, becoming even more crowded than usual. This was partially because of the bride—neighbors who had heard she was an *Oyibo* woman came to witness her arrival. What was supposed to be a somewhat small gathering had turned into a festival of more than five hundred people. Of course, the landlord was pleased—it was an opportunity for his family to brag about their son mingling with an *Oyibo* woman. We grew up seeing whiteness as some idolized form, the best way to live life. White people were portrayed in our culture and media as more successful, more educated. The *Oyibo* ways of life were thought of as more formal, more proper. This was constantly reinforced by television shows and movies we watched, the songs we sang, and the poems we recited in school. We understood that a white person was held in high regard, that words carried meaning. Because they were considered more successful than Africans, it was something of a status symbol to be seen with a white person. Our landlord's son has gone beyond mingling to marrying one.

When she arrived, the crowd was so large I could barely see her. I asked my elder sister to carry me on her shoulders to better see as she stepped out of a Toyota Camry. She was a slight woman of medium height, wearing gold high-heeled sandals and a white scarf covering her hair. Amid the roar of the cheering crowd, I mostly saw her back as she turned into the building. Indeed, this was the first time I would see a white person in the flesh—at that time, I had only seen white people on television. I felt important in her presence, civilized in a sense. I started arranging people in my mind across an invisible line—those who had seen a real white person and those who had not.

I knew my best way to see her again would be to cling close to my mum, as she would be among the women to dress her for the ceremony. When I asked my mum to bring me inside with her, she looked at me like I'd asked something unforgiveable. *Dig a hole in the floor and bury yourself in it*, her eyes said. Yet, I persisted, staring right back at her. She smiled, lowered her back, and told me to jump on her shoulders.

Our landlord's living room was packed with elders. When my mother lowered herself to drop me down, the elders leered at me, all of us knowing this was no place for a young boy. Nonetheless, I snuck past them, into the room where my mum would dress the bride.

She was sitting on the mattress, clearly shocked by the number of beads she had to wear. I felt sorry for her—she would have to change clothes three times during the ceremony. My mother was in her element, tying the *gele* around the bride's hair. I was intrigued by the ambiance of the room; I was more comfortable being in the company of women discussing their clothes and shoes than being in spaces where toxic masculinity overwhelmed the conversations. I felt perfectly natural among the loving and caring energy of women, even at this age.

As it was time for her to change further, the women asked me to leave, so the bride could have her privacy. But before I left, I asked if I could kiss her hand. She looked surprised. What was special about her? her face seemed to ask. Still, she offered me her hands before the women in the room could complain.

I kissed her hand; she held mine, tightly, and reciprocated.

With her lipstick mark on my hands, I ran to my elder sister outside to show her. The other kids gazed on with fondness. An *Oyibo* had kissed my hand! The bride's kiss on my hand meant so much more than a kiss—it signified my mingling with a superior race. This would be the talk of the town for days.

Growing up, "racism" was not a common word for an ordinary Nigerian. We argued over tribes and religious beliefs, but we were all the same, in that we were all Africans. We were taught to believe in the exceptionalism of whiteness, particularly in the Western world. We described the West as "the white man's world." We would say that in a white man's land, you could speak about your government without fear. In a white man's land, there were good roads, constant electricity, and they earned what they labored for.

Whites were better in every way. We were taught to believe that a white person's racism toward an African was the fault of the African—our lack of decency, our lack of education. But consider, Africans were intentionally not taught to read by our white colonizers due to their belief that this would displace the imbalance of power between them and the natives. We have internalized this thinking as Africans. (Once, in my English class in middle school, our class teacher, who clearly was a dark-skinned Nigerian, said: "The best place to hide your precious materials is in the library, because the African man does not read.") This was a phrase used by the colonizers and was now part of the vocabulary used by Nigerians. After Nigeria gained independence in the 1960s, part of building our relationships with the United Kingdom, the United States, and Western nations, was for Nigerian students to attend foreign colleges, with the notion and idea that they'd return to Nigeria to "rebuild" the country. But largely, students who studied abroad did not return, and those that did came back armed with a Western approach: how to talk, how to dress, and how to act. We gradually adopted a Western mindset for approaching our society and education—a subtle but very effective way of exporting Western culture.

Inherent to much of African social norms, though, is a sense of racist ideologies toward what "civilized culture" looks and sounds like—how to greet your masters, how to care for your family, how to prioritize education, no challenging of Western ideals, African traditional clothing, hairstyles, mannerisms, and grooming. What newly minted Western graduates did *not* return with was stories of how Americans and Europeans treated and are treating Black folks who live there. They did not talk about the discrimination and oppression of Black people. I did not know about slavery in the United States, the bus boycott, the march on Washington—these stories did not often travel back with them. All the stories about the United States we heard were about their beautiful college campuses and access to electricity, water, and good roads.

The only place where I have seen something closely related to discrimination and racism as a child was through the lens of African soccer players in Europe playing in major soccer leagues. Noon on Saturdays was when I'd watch English soccer with my father and elder brother. As distressed as the country had been since we gained independence, soccer was one thing that united the country. The Nigerian national team came from every part of the country; they spoke different languages and practiced different religions. I had no choice but to be a soccer fan—soccer is a part of life for a Nigerian and a Warri boy. I could easily recite the names of the twenty teams in the British premier soccer league. Learning the names of the players and understanding the game was an opportunity for me to bond with the only two men in my life, even though I was uncomfortable in these male spaces.

Top African soccer players were bought by big European teams—this was where they would be seen by the world and get paid in a higher foreign currency and live a comfortable life. But even in soccer there was a lingering sense of racism, if not from the players themselves, then from my father. He would always call the strong African players "blacky," because they'd play defense and retrieved the ball. White players passed smoothly and were intelligent strikers; Black players defended, according to my father, because they were not as smart. I recall that Samuel Eto'o of Cameroon was booed by white people in Barcelona, London, and France; he was a very intelligent striker, but he got pelted with banana peels, and on one of the occasions he had to be removed from the pitch for his own safety. Despite the fact that he helped his team win medals, he was despised for no other reason than for his Black skin. Talented African players cut their careers short, some of them moving to countries outside the European league. And beyond the field, the media also portrayed whiteness with nuance; there were the advertisements—the ads for cosmetics, especially, promoted a standard of white beauty in Nigeria that skyrocketed the sales of skin-whitening creams.

But it was also during these games that my father instilled in us the ideals of the West—their medicine, education, their general way of life. As an impressionable young boy, I began to fall in love with the West—to be a better man, I'd have to behave in the way of white Westerners. While I maybe began to see Europeans' racism—they had colonized the world, after all, and yet seemed to push Black people out of all arenas of life—I had yet to hear much of America's. Due to the time zones, it was hard to watch American sports—nor did we have baseball or American football—but I did have plenty of exposure to movies, television, and music. I began to admire Black people living in America, even if my exposure was limited to portrayals like Eddie Murphy in *Coming to America*, or Kerry Washington's Olivia Pope on *Scandal*, rappers like Tupac Shakur, and even CNN's Don Lemon, one of the first openly gay Black news anchors. Seeing these figures—Black people living successfully, even celebrated—helped establish the abiding narrative in my mind: Americans were good people, whereas Europeans were bad.

My generation grew up steeped and immersed in American and Western culture thanks to the invention of the internet. I grew up in the YouTube years at the peak of online culture as American teens flocked to the World Wide Web with their camera phones. Not only did this help to expand and expose broader cultural understandings, but it specifically gave me a sense of belonging. As a closeted gay boy in Nigeria, I found Facebook groups filled with American teens. Their conversations sometimes bordered on fetishizing; I wonder now if this helped lead me to believe America was the most welcoming place for a Black person such as myself.

When I had to flee Nigeria, I had few English-speaking countries to choose from. Australia was too far. And I had seen the British colonize, enslave, and trade Black folks, not to mention the racism I plainly saw on the soccer pitch each weekend; but America had Michael Jordan and Serena Williams, Carl Lewis and Arthur Ashe. Never mind that I was entirely ignorant to America's relationship with race, their own history of slavery and modern police brutality. This may have been obvious to people in the United States and Europe or even the rest of the world, but for me, growing up, it was never discussed or portrayed.

It wasn't until I arrived in America that I came to understand it was no safe haven—not only as a gay man, but as a Black gay man.

In 2017 after I got released from the detention center—when I had no job and was still living at the YMCA while waiting for my social security card to be activated—there were only a few places where I could spend my time. One of them was Newark Penn Station in New Jersey.

One morning, I found myself in the flock of early-morning commuters. Most of them were dressed formally, wearing suits and carrying briefcases—the uniform of the white working class. I was among those who roamed about the station, looking at stores, using the public restroom, and having a cup of coffee while Americans went on their way. It rained heavily on this day, so I stayed longer than expected.

As I approached the front door of the station, I knew I could not afford to get wet and fall sick with no medical insurance to see a doctor. Folks were waiting outside under the shelter, so I moved slightly to the side. It was then that I spotted a group of guys chatting with each other—one of them, a Black man, began to approach.

"Can I help you?" I asked. He was close enough that I could smell a foul stench on his breath. He remained silent, so I began stepping back slightly toward the door.

This was when he yelled at me, "Go back to your country, you bloody Haitian!" He launched into a vicious rant about how a Haitian had killed his brother.

"But I am not Haitian," I reassured him.

"Go back to where you came from," he said again, "or I will deal with you myself."

I was not only afraid but also confused. The guy then walked back to his friends, and I quickly ran into the rain toward the market.

The rain was pouring down hard, and as I walked slowly back toward the YMCA, I found myself crying. I had never witnessed people avoiding me in public spaces because I'm Black—or worse yet, confront me in public spaces because I'm Black. Another Black person had just told me to return to my country. What should I have called this? Racism or xenophobia? Today I might have had a calm conversation with him and explained that I wasn't from Haiti, but back then my days were characterized by a fear of the unknown.

When told to return to my country, what I would have wanted to say is that a refugee has no country. We lose that the day we leave.

In America, protectionism is tied to racism—we are told that foreign-born Black people are from Third World or underdeveloped countries when we arrive. The rejection of Black immigrants is tied to the perception of where we are coming from. When a Black person arrives in America, no matter their country of origin, their identity and race take on a different meaning. To a white person who would see me on the street, I was a Black man; to the Black men born in America, I was a foreigner, and perhaps not "authentically" Black. The definition of Blackness in America is a concept I have spent years trying to figure out and unpack, and one that I may not even fully understand as yet. Any American who visits Nigeria is not considered white or Black; they are all considered Americans. When a Black person travels to America, he may be Haitian or Nigerian, but first and foremost, he is Black—and that carries a very specific context for Americans.

Black people in America, regardless of nationality, are being killed for just being alive. As an immigrant, I fled my country for being gay. Although gay rights in America are progressing, we're still grappling with race and racism. While I am not African American—and my people were not slaves in early colonial America—I still tussle with slavery's legacy as a Black man in America. The stereotypes and prejudices from slavery have been built into not only how white Americans view Black Americans, but also how Black Americans view each other. The reality of living as a Black person is not having the option to choose how you would be perceived. To be good, to succeed in America, I saw, was to adopt whiteness in all its form. In my home country of Nigeria, I had to ask myself how should I get dressed this morning based on my sexual orientation; now I have to ask myself how

I dress based on my race. Will this outfit (e.g., wearing a hoodie) get me killed? This worry extends beyond what to wear—we must also think about how to act in public spaces. Think of Trayvon Martin, whose crime was wearing a hoodie at night. Think of Tamir Rice, whose crime was playing with a toy gun in a park. Think of Ahmaud Arbery, whose crime was jogging in daylight. In private, we must worry too. Think of Breonna Taylor, whose crime was being asleep.

In reality, their crimes were existing with Black skin. Am I next? This is the question almost every Black person—especially Black men—ask themselves when another unarmed Black person is shot by the police.

Policing in America affects Black immigrant communities, too. In 2020, one in ten Black people living in America emigrated from another country.* Racial stereotypes begin at the border—border patrol agents use racial profiling to detain immigrants of color; but even beyond the border, heavy policing of majority Black neighborhoods has led to higher arrest and detainment rates of Black immigrants over other groups.†

Even the immigration system has begun favoring criminalizing Black people who might have a minor crime on their record.

* Monica Anderson and Gustavo López, "Key Facts about Black Immigrants in the U.S.," Pew Research Center, January 24, 2018, https://www.pewresearch.org/fact-tank/2018/01/24/key-facts-about-black-immigrants-in-the-u-s; Abby Budiman, "Key Findings about U.S. Immigrants," Pew Research Center, August 20, 2020, https://www.pewresearch.org/fact-tank/2020/08/20/key-findings-about-u-s-immigrants/

† RAICES, https://www.raicestexas.org/2020/07/22/black-immigrant-lives-are-under-attack/; Brad Heath, "Racial Gap in U.S. Arrest Rates: 'Staggering Disparity,'" *USA Today*, November 18, 2014, https://www.usatoday.com/story/news/nation/2014/11/18/ferguson-black-arrest-rates/19043207/.

Obama became known as the "Deporter-in-Chief" for focusing his immigration efforts toward deeming those with criminal backgrounds as unsafe to immigrate to America. But things changed during the Trump administration. If a Black immigrant was charged for a minor crime such as possession of marijuana, they could be placed into a detention center after being released from prison. U.S.-born citizens facing the same charges would serve time and be reinstated into society. Black immigrants, though, could be sent back to the country they'd fled.

In 2019 I was invited to a synagogue on the Upper West Side of Manhattan as a guest speaker to discuss immigration. I was dressed casually in pants and a shirt, nothing fancy. When I got to the event venue I was greeted by the security at the front door. When she asked me what I was looking for, I told her I was attending the immigrant event hosted at the synagogue. She looked at her papers and said there is no event here tonight.

Soon after, two white women walked in and said they were here for an immigration event. She allowed them in. I tried to clarify, that I was the guest speaker for the event those women were attending. She still refused me entry.

I called the event organizers—who were white—to explain what was happening. They came outside to meet me at the door, apologized, and guided me inside, assuring me that the guard would be reprimanded.

This was one of the more troubling instances—to be barred entry from an event where I was the guest of honor—but these aggressions happen on a macro and micro scale. My partner is white—when we go out to restaurants, I am often asked to show ID, whereas he is not.

I have always challenged the prejudice people have toward me, but it is an exhausting responsibility to educate your discriminators. I have only lived in America for a few years, and it is already exhausting—I've often wondered how African Americans have lived with these issues for their entire lives.

But I'm not only Black, I am also gay. As a Black gay man, I have found myself torn—I am free to be gay in America, but I am not sure how free I am to be Black. I fled my country for being gay; where do I run for protection from being Black?

I can only relate my experiences of Blackness in America to those of my experiences of queerness in Nigeria. Police brutality in America targets Blacks—in Nigeria, they target gay people. Gay people are often falsely accused of crimes and harassed, simply for being suspected of being gay. Stop-and-search techniques—not dissimilar to New York City Mayor Bloomberg's racially pointed stop-and-frisk policies—are widely used in major cities such as Lagos, Port Harcourt, and Abuja. Police would set up checkpoints, stopping effeminate men, going as far as to search their bags for pornography or their phone for gay dating apps. Even having a photo of yourself in close proximity to another man—let alone kissing or hugging—is suspect.

The police use being gay as a tool to exploit suspected gay men. Being Black in America means having no privacy either, having every small aspect of your life—from your clothes to your accent—scrutinized, as was true of my experience of being gay in Nigeria.

I have found some common ground in understanding the Black American experience through migration for fear of violence. Just as the Underground Railroad was designed to deliver people to safer territory, queer people—especially queer people of color—turn to similar modern versions of this migration pattern. The Canadian organization Rainbow Railroad helps queer immigrants fleeing violence get access to flight tickets, visas, and financial support to flee to a safer country; even their organization name harkens to the historical necessity for flight to safety. But even after being delivered to safety in America, it was clear not all spaces were safe—if not for my Blackness, then for my queerness.

It's a complicated dance to be gay and Black in America, no matter where you hail from. I have seen that the African American community and Afro Latino community are not as accepting of gay people. Working as the empowerment officer for Hyacinth AIDS Foundation, many young people I worked with were Black LGBTQ people facing rejection from their families and friends. Many of them struggled to accept their sexuality. It was very hard to be faced with the same interactions I had with my family in Africa. I tried to guide them by using my life as an example—I fled to America to truly be who I am, and I didn't see any reason why they could not be themselves in America too. What I failed to recognize, even then, was that I had paid a great price.

I have not been back to Nigeria in five years. When I told my mother that I fled because of who I am, I meant every word of it. I am sure she came from a place of love, as any mother tries to, but I could not engage with her *if*s and *but*s. My family still has trouble reconciling my sexuality; they still believe the day I find God I will stop sleeping with men. I may be freer here, but I have paid the price of contact with the people who raised me, the people I still love. My early days in this country showed me quickly how naïve I was. In the small gay community of New Jersey, I was hardly accepted. Despite the legal battles that have been won in court, being an openly gay Black immigrant in America, I saw, was a radical act of self-acceptance.

Isolated, I often tried turning to Sylvester, my gay, Black, immigrant ally. When I would ask him to hang out with me, he would refuse due to attending a church filled with folks in the diaspora community. They did not accept gay people, and being caught—even in America!—would risk his safety and acceptance with some of the only people he could rely on. In my work, I turned to speaking about my sexuality through online advocacy, but even this grew isolating. Africans wanted nothing to do with me. As a new immigrant, I imagined I'd be able to seek refuge and understanding from other gay people, at LGBTQ centers or even at bars and clubs. In my early days, visiting a center in downtown Manhattan, I found very few people to speak to—mostly the center was filled with teens struggling to reconcile their sexuality, but I was in a different leg of my journey. The bars were filled with people—mostly white—who knew each other through friends of friends of friends. It was like I had lost an invitation to a party I probably wasn't invited to. As a child of the internet, turning to gay dating apps was the next logical step.

I did find people to sleep with, but often these people wanted me because of (racist) perceptions—that I was sexually strong because I was Black. I remember the first time someone on an app asked if I had BBC. At first, I thought he meant the British Broadcasting Channel; he said, no, a big Black cock. As an HIV/AIDS worker in New Jersey, I was often stunned by how many people tried to have unprotected sex, a concept that was totally in opposition to how I had behaved in Nigeria due to the prevalence of the disease. Worse yet, a man once asked me to be his "slave"—whether this was purely sexual, it's hard to ignore the fact that, in this country, there was plainly a painful history with that word and my race. Imagine coming from a country where you are criminalized for being gay and not for being Black, to arriving in a country where you realize your identity as a Black person defines almost everything about you, even in queer spaces. As an immigrant of color, your experience is shaped through the color of your identity; as a queer person of color, doubly so. I am always a *Black* gay man, never just a gay man.

In Nigeria, sex was quick—I was used to spending five minutes, in and out, often due to fear of being caught. I hoped in America, I could afford myself time in safety—that I could have the opportunity to explore sex and sexuality, without fear of repercussions. Americans, I saw, had adapted a quick and easy attitude toward sex—if not for fear of safety than because of an abundance of safety. Sex was sometimes even quicker in America. You could have multiple partners in one day if you wanted; you could have a quick five-minute hookup on your way home from the gym before meeting a friend for dinner. There was a casualness and urgency to sex, and sometimes I feared it was due to my partners not wanting to be caught in the act with an immigrant (from Africa, no less). I was troubled by the lack of spaces for queer people who migrated to New York, to meet other queer immigrants in the diaspora.

By my second year in America, already the director of the RDJ Refugee Shelter, I decided to finally attend a Pride event. I did not know who to join, so I joined the Immigration Equality float, made up of many immigrants of color. We gathered at Chelsea to march together, and during the march I spotted a man I knew to be a queer in Nigeria. I ran toward him to take a picture, thinking it would be nice to document us together proudly celebrating.

"No!" he said forcefully, and then looking embarrassed, he said again, more softly, "No, no. I just came here to watch. Please." Stunned, I said, "Of course," and returned to the march. It was hard not to feel ashamed, but I stayed fixated on the fact that this man had fled violence to live safely and freely here in America, yet still he felt he had to hide in the shadows. Was he so different from Sylvester? And could I blame them? Look at how difficult I found it, still, to be queer in America; look at how my family and community back home still couldn't accept me even if I could.

By the end of the day, I was grateful I attended the event. There was something so beautiful about seeing people of all stripes and colors marching together, united under a single cause and hope. I may not have known all the people personally, but I felt more at home, more buoyed by seeing my community rally together. Since the man from the crowd wouldn't take a picture with me, I took a selfie at the event and uploaded it to social media. Quickly, many so-called African friends in America asked me to take the photo down. I was being "too loud" about this "gay thing." This was my constant bargain—to have a relationship with the African diaspora community meant conforming to a Nigerian way of life in America. Go with them to church on Sundays, don't act too gay—don't act gay at all, even—and never step outside their circle of influence, or face being outcast. I may have been a gay Black man in America, but to my community of fellow immigrants, mentally, we should have all acted like we were still at home.

Nicholas and I met on the popular gay dating app, Grindr. We couldn't be more different, at first glance. He is a tall Italian American who grew up on Long Island; I am anything but that. I met Nicholas during a time of great struggle—I felt isolated from my communities, had few friends, and certainly no confidants. I did have Cristina, though, and we were drinking in her apartment when his message came in. My first thought was *Here we go again, another white boy.* I told Cristina, and she laughed—but she encouraged me to keep chatting, keep trying. We talked for a while, and I decided to give him the pet name of Nicky Minaj before we exchanged numbers. Though because Cristina and I had been drinking, I didn't realize I hadn't shared this pet name with him.

When we spoke on the phone for the first time, just a bit later, I said, "Hello, Nicky Minaj," when he picked up.

"I think you have the wrong number?" he said.

"No," I said. "That's you. You're Nicky Minaj." He laughed, and I gestured to Cristina that he seemed into it.

We finally agreed to meet that evening for a drink. I had no intention except to have fun. We went to a bar in Brooklyn to play pool and have a drink. When we got there the bar was filled, all the pool tables were taken, so instead we grabbed seats at the bar and began chatting. Meeting Nicholas felt different from other guys I had met. He was a bit shy and drawn into himself.

"Tell me about yourself," he said. Where to begin? I started at the beginning, as best I could, and even as pool tables freed up, we kept chatting. Pretty soon, the bar was closing.

We went to his place that night. If I was living in Nigeria, Nicholas would have been a one-night stand, because we could not have continued seeing each other without drawing suspicion. My experiences in New York led me to think Nicholas would be another one-night stand anyway—that seemed to be how things worked here. When I left in the morning, after not hearing back from me for a few hours, he called me and asked me out a second time. This was quite unusual. Was I free to see a movie later?

I was.

Nicholas helped shift my perspective. Quiet and a bit serious, he was unlike the other gay men I'd met in New York, who seemed more obsessed with the gay scene, and themselves, to really care about the real person on the other side of the bed. We dated for a few months before he asked me if I would go meet his family out on Long Island.

Before Nicholas, I had never had a visible gay relationship. Nicholas may have been shy, but he had brought a boyfriend home before. His family was open and accepting of his sexuality, having come out in his teen years. The proposition seemed nice, but a bit rushed—and the movie *Get Out* had just hit theaters recently. I joked about that, which made him laugh. "No," he said. "My family is really excited to meet you."

Nicholas had told his family I was Black, and a refugee, to prepare them. He told me they skewed a bit "right wing" but reassured me that had nothing to do with accepting their only son. I met his family in waves, first traveling to Northport to his elder sister's place, where she entertained us in her lovely living room. We were shortly joined by his younger sister next.

Danielle, Nick's elder sister, asked me how I was doing. Did I want a drink?

I did.

Nick's younger sister, Gabby, asked me what I did for a living.

We had little to say to each other because Nick had warned me before we got there not to talk about politics. When you identify as an activist, people judge you before you utter a word. The notion of me being someone that stands for something does not mean I cannot hold a conversation outside my views.

I replied to Gabby, without flinching, "I work with refugees in New York, helping homeless people find access to housing." The nice and easy way to say it would have been, I work for a nonprofit organization, but I could not stop myself from making it clear who I am by what I do.

The next stop would be a family wedding in Ocean City, where I would meet his mom, stepdad, and the rest of his family. When we arrived, it all changed. I found it a bit shocking—everyone lived in their own building, with their own garages, totally uncrowded. This was nothing like my place in Manhattan, let alone Warri, or even Abuja.

At the wedding venue, guests began piling in. I looked for another Black person—even just one—but it became clear that of the hundred or so guests, I was the only one. These were two large Italian American families on Long Island, after all. And their son had shown up with his date, a Black, gay refugee. I soon met Nicholas's mum, stepdad, and extended family. I did not have much time to speak to each member of the family, but his mum approached with a pretty smile and jewelry dangling from her as she bent toward me to kiss my cheek. "Welcome," she said warmly. She seemed excited to meet me, but we had all been drinking, so it was hard to tell. I never felt excluded, they were very welcoming, and I even had the opportunity to have a dance with Nicholas as one of the only interracial and one of the few gay couples at the wedding.

We had a great night and drove back home to spend the rest of the weekend at Danielle's place. She also made us aware she would be holding her birthday this summer and she would like Nicholas to bring me along with him. Shortly after, I started bringing Nicholas around to meet my friends.

Nicholas always seemed like he was trying to impress me with food—we'd go to French and Italian restaurants with unimaginable prices. When it was my turn to pick, I took him to a Thai restaurant in Jackson Heights and our total bill was less than forty dollars—but we ended that night at a Venezuelan bar playing bingo with the elderly.

"So this is where you like to spend your time," he asked with a slightly joking tone.

"It's where I feel like I belong," I told him. But it wasn't all bingo—I would occasionally get to bring him to a decadent fundraiser or charity event.

Eventually, the day came that I realized I was in love with him—he had rented a U-Haul to drive me to Ikea in Brooklyn to help me furnish my new apartment, even though I knew he hated to shop. If you've ever been to the Ikea in Brooklyn, you know this is the place where relationships are tested.

In my extremely hot apartment, I stayed behind to assemble my new Ikea bed while Nicholas ran to P.C. Richard to buy me a new air conditioner. "A housewarming gift," he said. "Or, house-cooling." Was I dreaming?

Though I love Nicholas, our relationship has not been easy—not necessarily because of us, but because of the world around us. It's challenging to be in an interracial relationship, let alone a gay one. The Nigerians I know thought I was just with Nicholas because he's wealthy and white—that it was a relationship of upward mobility for me. One of Nicholas's friends is dating a Black guy. The guy posted on social media one day that "Black people are selling out for dating white people, they are betraying our ancestors and will rot in the hottest parts of hell." I showed Nick the post and he admitted he'd also faced pushback. "People don't understand why I'm dating an African immigrant," he told me, explaining that one of his closest white friends used to date an African from Ghana, and said he was only doing so because the guy needed a place to live. When Nick became my partner, I had unanswered questions. Would people think I was chasing some white man for his wealth?

The legalization of gay marriage in 2015 meant that I could freely love who I wanted to in America. My relationship with Nicholas has become an integral part of my life. I have a renewed sense of meaning because I have a family in him; he has shown me what commitment and love can look and feel like. This makes it worth whatever adversity we face.

In December of 2018, Nick took me on my first skiing trip to Upstate New York. I was excited to try something new, but nervous. I was that dot of blackness on a white peak. I wanted to just sit out and watch, but Nicholas asked me to join him at the bunny hills; even if I couldn't ski, we could still take some pictures. On the bunny hill, I fell over constantly, while kids easily skied by me. But I found myself unashamed—I was trying something new. I would rather be laughed at for not being able to ski, than to be laughed at for skiing with another man.

An instructor came over to us and said with a laugh, "This must be your first time."

I nodded. She asked where I was from.

"Nigeria," I replied.

"Oh," she said, "you guys have a lot of snow there!"

We both laughed. She told Nicholas he could leave, that she would keep watch over me, so Nicholas went to get in some skiing. I tried once or twice but could only ski about a mile or so without falling.

As I packed up my gear near the office, I saw Nicholas stuck up on the mountain. "Do you need help?" I yelled. He shook his hands and head no, no, no.

I walked inside the locker room, changed out of my ski clothes, and sat waiting for him to finish, but he was taking longer than I expected. I walked outside, and there was Nicholas a little further down the slope, but clearly in need of help. In his defense, the slopes were very icy that day. I ran up to help him down.

That year I spent Christmas Eve with Nick's family. By then, his mother had warmed to me more, and is one of the sweetest women you will find on Long Island, or anywhere. She greeted us with open arms, and even bought gifts for me to celebrate the holiday. It was lovely—and it made me wish my own family back in Nigeria might one day support us, would one day be as welcoming to their gay son as Nicholas's family has been to me and him.

Nicholas and I were not meant to be together by the standards of the society we live in, but we have worked to be together. There were instances of objection from within the gay community, but as gay people, we face strain from the world at large. At first, Nicholas could not see these clues. Sometimes when we'd go out to eat, I'd ask Nicholas to let me pay. I would give my card to the waiter, and they would return the check to Nicholas to sign. Another time, at a restaurant, I ordered a steak well-done. It was delivered to me burnt. I tried to complain to the waiter, but he would only speak to Nicholas. This was when Nicholas started to see what I was talking about. Too often I have had to suppress my voice—or have had my voice suppressed—for being gay, for being Black, for being an immigrant, or for being all three.

Frankly speaking, the following story is not one I ever hoped to tell, but I owe it to the people that have come before me and the ones who will come after me. There is an implicit bias imbedded in how we assess any situation we are given to analyze, based on the unconscious stimulation from our environment and society at large. When I left the detention center, I had the opportunity to network on LinkedIn and other social networking sites. Oftentimes when I meet a new person, we chat online and we agree to meet. At first these meetings seem genuine and involve older, more experienced queer people inviting me to their office or a coffee shop for a meetup. One of the people I met was an older white guy who asked me to come for a coffee and maybe take a tour of his office.

The day of the meeting, I wanted to impress. I dressed up in the nicest shoes I had. He met me at the coffee shop and offered to pay for my coffee. *What a nice gesture*, I thought. When I got to his office, he closed the door and began telling me private details of his personal life. He put his arm on my shoulder, and I felt uncomfortable. I stood up immediately and told him I would have to leave.

Since that day, whenever I meet an older gay guy, a mentor, or people with good intentions, I tell them about my previous experience with this man. I intentionally present the facts of my relationship and talk about my partner to protect myself. Immigrants who are in need of help and find themselves in this sort of situation are sometimes exploited in exchange for being provided with support. I was in a vulnerable position; I needed the connection and support, but my integrity was also important to me.

I believe there are many well-meaning people out there; I am lucky to have met one. Nicholas has shown consistently that he is willing to learn, grow with me, and fight the battle together. Many people are not capable of giving the support needed to navigate difficulties. I have to plan many months ahead when I travel because I have to apply for a refugee travel document. There are many countries I cannot travel to at all. My mental health is unstable; I suffer from PTSD. I have found myself guilty of pushing Nicholas away, feeling unworthy of his love. My life's work in activism often means that Nicholas has had to stand up to close friends and family in order to protect the person he loves.

Eleven years ago, when I came out to my grandmother, I did not know what the future held for me. I never knew I would one day live in a society where I could be free enough to conceive of the idea of being in a relationship. Yet here I am, despite the trials of fleeing my home and coming to start afresh in America.

Living in New York, meeting kindhearted strangers one after the other, becoming friends, getting to know Nicholas, has made me hopeful. We live in an imperfect world, but I would do it all over again to meet the people I have met, in this life I have built, and those I am yet to meet.

It's with that same hope that I write this. Nicholas and I will be getting married one day. We will build a family. We will fight for equality, together. We can do this because of the hard work and effort of people who came before us, people who sacrificed their lives to ensure our rights as interracial gay folks who want to be together. I carry that hope with me in my relationship. I carry that hope with me in my work for a better future.

I always tell him how proud I am to be in an interracial relationship. I believe our love is a radical activism, challenging the concept of love beyond our skin color.

But that ideal was upended after the shooting of Daunte Wright, a young man born to interracial parents who was killed by police during a traffic stop. I realized we can build a mixed-race family and still face the persecution that many people of color face in America.

CHAPTER FIVE

Faith in America and West Africa

Sexuality and race have been prisms through which I've considered what it means to find freedom as an immigrant in America. For me—and for many immigrants—faith has been another. To pray among believers—however you identify—is to witness power in community. Houses of worship, the converging place for people of faith, should be a place for community; purity is not the *standard*, but the *ideal worshippers* seek purity when we gather and listen to a preacher delivering a sermon.

I grew up in a Pentecostal church and consider myself a true believer of Christ. I revered religious leaders, and the sanctimony of the position they held, and I became a minister myself. Still to this day the fundamental beliefs of Christianity are ingrained in me. I wouldn't be the person I am today if not for the teachings the Bible bestowed upon me—stories of resilience and standing up for what is right. In Nigeria and many religious communities, there is the belief in purity—community is created by doing good, harming no one, and following the scriptures so as to be rewarded on earth and in heaven. It is only natural that I have been trained to view life through a lens of purity.

My community revered priests, pastors, and people who were considered messengers of God. In most communities, the religious leaders were the only ones who could read and write. Ministers helped congregants to write letters to their children in the cities, and because of this, they knew almost everything about their lives. I aspired and strived to be that person, leading the flock of Christ, because it brought respect. Despite the church telling me I had no place within it as a gay person, Christians strive to be saint-like, lovers of all humankind—but man has created limitations to a certain few because of who they choose to love or based on factors defined by man. Even my own grandmother, a fervent believer, always told me God loves everyone and seeks to unite all. Love is all we yearn for, to love and be loved. LGBTQ people have eagerly sought opportunities to belong, but the church continually builds walls instead of bridges. My quest as a person of faith has been to uncover what faith means to us all—especially those of us who have not been invited in because of how we identify.

In retrospect, the courage I found to come out to my grandmother was rooted in my faith. My faith had taught me to be brave, to be upright and truthful—yet my faith also made me an outsider once I came out. The fear of God was instilled in me—but to seek this God in a house that has not welcomed me is the dilemma I have tried reconciling all my life and am still trying to reconcile today.

I became a pastor believing it would be a shield to protect me from the constant queries from family and friends on my relationship status or stop my attraction to other men by being a fervent Christian. Instead, churches and religion became a tool I used to inflict pain on myself, listening to ministers preach about my place in hell, constantly dehumanizing anyone who identified as gay. Though I had to abandon the church in Nigeria, through my journeys both geographical and personal, the teaching of the Bible kept me rooted in the radical belief that anything is possible—as was true for David, the underdog, who killed Goliath.

My relationship with the church as an institution has changed over the years, but my faith as a believer has remained strong, even as it has shifted. I believe I have succeeded in my work and in my life partially because I've learned what it means to have faith in something other than myself.

To have faith is not to sit in a house of worship, sing and dance, and pay a portion of your salary into tithes. It does not mean, as it often did in the Pentecostal-influenced style of religion in Nigeria, attending amusement park–styled ceremonies with ministers casting out demons from within, or putting on theatrical displays.

My immigration lawyer, Mrs. Ross, once told me after my asylum hearing that the universe tended to work in our favor; it listens to what we speak to it. Prayer is putting your words out in the universe and the universe telegraphing it back to you. The universe answering you back, however obvious or not, to me, is a prayer.

The people who have come along my journey to help me, guide me, pray with me, advise me, represent me, donate their time and energy to the cause, I believe, have been the universe answering my prayers. That is the faith I have found: coming to

America with no plan, believing there will be a way, strangers becoming friends, friends becoming family.

Having faith—religious faith or otherwise—has been a commonality for me and many others. I do not care what tribe you belong to or what local language you speak: if you are a Christian, you are my brother or sister. Nigeria being a multicultural nation meant the only commonality I might have shared with people from other tribes and backgrounds was their religion. Faith has helped collapse the walls between me and others. On Sunday morning, wherever I found myself, I knew I would have community in a nearby church where I could walk in, sing hymns together, pray together, and share in grace. Nothing can compare to the family you create when you share bread with a stranger. But my sexuality has made it difficult to reconcile the communion I get from breaking bread with strangers, and the constant negativity I felt inside houses of worship. I did not feel the same sense of community walking out as I did walking in, after hearing at length about the sins of my identity.

When I began learning about my sexuality in my teen years, I had to suppress my identity and sexuality to belong to a religious community that believed me to be demonic. If I ever mentioned I was gay out loud, they'd think I was possessed. Citations such as Leviticus 18:22: *You shall not lie with a male as with a woman; it* is *abomination*, and Leviticus 20:13: *They shall surely be put to death; and their blood* shall be *upon them*, have been used by religious folks in West Africa to directly attack and ostracize gay people. Religion has become a weapon, but this is hardly a modern convention in Africa. The demonization of gay people in Africa dates to colonial times—homosexuality is not a new phenomenon, but the demonization of homosexuality began when colonizers used religion as a means of enforcing "traditional" versions of family. This idea of making homosexuality un-African was a propaganda tool. Prior to the European invasion of Africa and other Indigenous lands, there were a vast spectrum of sexualities and gender identities.

In *Boys-Wives and Female Husbands*, a book which examines homosexuality and feminism in pre-colonial and colonial Africa, researchers found "Bushman artworks" that depict men engaging in same-sex activity.* In Northern Nigeria, *yan daudu* is a Hausa term for describing effeminate men who are considered wives to men.†

Colonization forcibly squeezed out any form of sexual or gender expression enjoyed by Africans and embedded the Western/European view of Christianity and Islam into the lives of Africans. The reason Africans now stigmatize homosexuality date as far back as the fight for domination of the land. The later Roman Empire wrote the first pieces of writings labeling Africa as a pure land free of this demonic sexual tension between the same gender.‡

Same-gender couples were in direct opposition to the stereotypical male/female roles that were set up on colonizing plantations. The logic was, if two couples of the same gender lived in the same household, who would be the "head" of that home? Who would work in the home, and who would work the land? In the

* Brockman, N. (2000). [Review of the book *Boy-Wives and Female Husbands: Studies of African Homosexualities*]. *Africa Today* 47(1), 153-155. doi:10.1353/at.2000.0005.

† http://www.arcados.ch/wp-content/uploads/2012/06/MURRAY-ROSCOE-BOY-WIVES-FEMALE-HUSBANDS-98.pdf.

‡ Afe Adogame, Ezra Chitando, and Bolaji Bateye, eds., *African Traditions in the Study of Religion, Diaspora and Gendered Societies* (London: Ashgate, 2013).

church, men were leaders and women were helpers—which echoed the same traditional Western gender roles colonizers brought to Africa. Further, the enslavement of Black people contributed to the demonization of homosexuality, as homosexuality posed a threat to labor; not only that, but also it threatened reproduction, a key factor in increasing the labor force. The demonization of homosexuality kept the colonizers and enslavers in power and popularized negative views of homosexuality on the continent of Africa. This extends beyond Africa—in the West, evangelicals have popularized the idea that a man is the head of the household, while a woman must nurture and care for the family.

When you have a conversation with an African about homosexuality, their burning question is always: "Are you the man or the woman?" Homosexuality is understood on a one-dimensional plane of the gender binary—who is the "man" and who is the "woman" in your relationship; these debates aren't concerned with love or emotion, the bedrocks of a healthy relationship. Growing up in the church, I often heard ministers use phrases such as, "God created humans to reproduce, and gay people are against God's plan for us humans." How can a God create us all and choose who to love and who to hate? If one of the greatest commandments Jesus taught was to love, love your God and love your neighbor as yourself, how can he make exceptions?

Religion has become a complicated, nuanced, and popular narrative in the denunciation and criminalization of same-sex relationships in Nigeria and across Africa. One can say religion is the driving force behind homophobia in Africa, portraying Christianity and LGBTQ expression as incompatible. From a very young age we internalized the idea that homosexuals are possessed—we were taught to mute any feelings you might nurture for a same-sex partner. Sometimes the only way to ward off any suspicious eyes was to become a supposedly fervent Christian—as I did. Being close to God as a form of showmanship might ward off suspicion.

In my interactions with Black people born in America, I have told them about my experience with religion in Africa, and they are shocked. African Americans I know have looked to the traditional religious practices in Africa to find understanding and acceptance outside of a Western context because the Black church often demonizes homosexuality. They are told their ancestors came from Africa, where homosexuality may have once been normalized, but has since been warped into an idea that homosexuality is "un-African." This has been especially true with the rise and popularization of conversion therapy throughout Africa and former British colonies around the world, including America, leading to widespread human rights abuses.

Religious Nigerians participate in conversion therapy in their houses of worship and in the north; Islamic Nigerians punish homosexuality with flogging. A person suspected of homosexuality will be tied to a rope and whipped with chains to cast out the demonic spirits. There is also widespread misinformation about HIV/AIDS and the gay community; characterizing gay men as pedophiles who will rot in hell has contributed to the dehumanization and stigmatization of queer people.

In modern times, more and more, however, Evangelicals in the West were losing their plight at home—so they have had to focus their energy on further importing their ideas and beliefs to Africa. Much of the anti-gay philosophy in Africa is funded by dark money. Dark money refers to religious organizations receiving tax deductible donations and using it to fuel harmful policies and influence political decisions. It is often funneled from the Western evangelical churches registered as 501(c)(3) not-for-profit organizations that are supposed to steward tax-free donations toward improving peoples' lives.

For example, in 2020, according to Pink News, Billy Graham's Evangelistic Association donated $96,132,520 from 2007 to 2014 to some of the largest funders of anti-gay Evangelical missions in Africa. More than twenty U.S. Christian groups known for fighting against LGBTQ rights and access to safe abortion, contraceptives, and comprehensive sexual education, have spent at least $54 million in Africa since 2007.*

In more recent years the Evangelicals have fueled anti-gay legislation. For example, in Zambia in 2012—the same year they won the prestigious African Cup of Nations in soccer—the UN High Commissioner for Human Rights visited, dominating the air waves. Her visit led to African leaders passing anti-gay legislation, in rebuke of Western influence in Africa. For example, this led to the Uganda "Kill the Gays" bill written by David Bahati, an associate of the secretive U.S. religious group, the Fellowship Foundation. Between 2008 and 2018, this group sent more than $20 million to Uganda alone to fund anti-gay legislation and propaganda campaigns against LGBTQ rights.†

* Ibid.

† Josh Milton, "Christian Groups Spent Hundreds of Millions in 'Dark Money' Waging War on LGBT+ and Women's Rights Around the World," PinkNews, October 28, 2020, https://www.pinknews.co.uk/2020/10/28/christian-far-right-dark-money-donald-trump-opendemocracy-bgea-adf-aclj-lgbt/.

Some LGBTQ Ugandans have courageously refused to stay silent and continued to fight for their human rights. This led to the death of human rights activist Brian Wasswa, who was found fatally wounded in his home and lying in a pool of his own blood on October 4, 2019. The propaganda was that Mr. Wasswa was possessed, and his death was punishment from God for his sins.* Shortly after his death, the Uganda parliament brought the bill to the house floor. In an interview with Reuters, Uganda Ethics and Integrity Minister Simon Lokodo said, "Homosexuality is not natural to Ugandans, but there has been a massive recruitment by gay people in schools, and especially among the youth, where they are promoting the falsehood that people are born like that . . . Our current penal law is limited. It only criminalizes the act. We want it made clear that anyone who is even involved in promotion and recruitment has to be criminalized. Those that do grave acts will be given the death sentence."†

The "Kill the Gays" bill has faced backlash from both Ugandan and international media, but despite this, it has created a ripple effect leading to other African countries passing anti-gay legislation.

Similarly, former president Barack Obama's 2014 visit to Africa led to further backlash. Obama's advocacy for human rights and fair treatment of LGBTQ persons led to African's viewing

* "Uganda: Brutal Killing of Gay Activist," *Human Rights Watch*, October 15, 2019, https://www.hrw.org/news/2019/10/15/uganda-brutal-killing-gay-activist#.

† Nita Bhalla, "Uganda Plans Bill Imposing Death Penalty for Gay Sex," Reuters, October 10, 2019, https://www.reuters.com/article/us-uganda-lgbt-rights/uganda-plans-bill-imposing-death-penalty-for-gay-sex-idUSKBN1WP1GN.

the West as promoting homosexuality. Evangelical groups and churches across Africa labeled Obama as an antichrist and agent of the devil. He canceled a trip to Nigeria because of the passage of the 2014 Same-Sex Marriage (Prohibition) Act by the Nigerian government, which criminalized same-sex relations. The language of this legislation, and others like it, is coded with influence to systematically label Africa God's land and cleanse the continent from the so-called Western influence of homosexuality on the continent of Africa.

Churches and Evangelical missions have shaped the language and conversation surrounding homosexuality, stoking fear of Westernization in Africa, the deconstruction of family values, labeling gays as pedophiles, and using diseases like HIV/AIDS as an explanation for punishment by a higher power.

Since religious rhetoric is so deeply tied to the discussion of gay rights, it has become difficult to argue with those who have deep-seated religious beliefs—which is much of the African population. But now is the time to change.

I am a preacher, not a pastor. My gospel is no longer the doctrines of the Bible but of humanity. I do not have to be a religious leader to teach about love. I do believe in God's love as many queer people do around the world, but I now preach self-love and an inherent love for one another. The work of changing people's minds does not only happen in houses of worship; it also happens in our day-to-day experiences. The same principles applied in houses of worship are what you feel when you attend a concert or watch a play—you feel moved and sometimes touched by the artist's performance. These transcendent experiences do not have to happen exclusively in churches—the world offers us many opportunities to broaden our worldviews and expand our perspectives. Doing so, I believe, is similar to the experience of finding faith in a higher calling or an extraordinary power that you cannot define.

Before I came to America, I had never met a Jewish person. I did not know Jewish people were still alive. It was during my time on the board of First Friends, in New Jersey, when I met Emily and learned she was Jewish. Through her I've learned more about other religions, and the way Jews embody a sense of welcoming to those who suffer persecution. Learning about Judaism has brought to light the limitations of my worldview, stemming from my upbringing as a Pentecostal Christian. As a result of my activism, I have had the opportunity to worship in different houses. What I've seen is that the unifying favor in all houses of worship is love.

In 2017 I was invited to speak at a church in New Jersey. I was not giving a sermon; rather I was to "preach" in the form of a speech, as part of an event put on by an immigrants' rights group. Flora, the pen pal of my friend Mohammed from the detention center, and her mother, Dorothy, attended the church. At first I was afraid to stand at an altar to speak about God's love for people—my relationship with the church had gone sour, and I worried people would not want to hear a gay man speak about his faith. Could you blame me, after the way the church in Nigeria had shunned me? At that point, I had not been to church since leaving the detention center months ago. I was afraid to revisit the Bible.

The reverend read a portion of the Bible and then called me to speak. I stood in front of the church and told my story of coming out in a church and being chased by my pastor. I spoke about my renewed faith in humanity because of the friends I had met while I was in detention; I went as far as to ask the congregation to practice God's message of love by visiting a detention center, or writing to someone in a center. The response was an overwhelming silence, but one that felt positive. I knew my message had sunk in—that Americans of all people were highly capable of granting kindness to strangers, as they had done for me.

Later, I was invited to another church, but this time to actually preach. It was a Pentecostal church in Boston. This felt like a bold step for me, as it had been years since I had given any type of sermon using the Bible. When I was released from the detention center, I had left my Bible there—at that time, I felt I was done with religion, that it had served its purpose carrying me through my imprisonment. I still did not own a Bible with which to prepare, so I turned to an internet Bible. Reading scriptures again felt like medicine—I've always been amazed by biblical stories offering philosophy for every aspect of life. Then, I found it difficult to pray. Yet now I had a new mindset, and a new message of love to help guide me. And I had Nick, who drove me to Boston. Nick grew up Catholic, but not that religious; and he was fascinated that I would be teaching in a church. He had never fashioned me a religious person.

In downtown Cambridge, as I stepped inside the church, I felt old feelings—of being in communion with God's children—return to me. I felt purified by the music and ambience. Inside the mostly empty church, I found my friend Tom, who had invited me. Tom showed me the Sunday bulletin then, which had included my name and bio, mentioning that I was a refugee from Nigeria, but no mention of my sexuality. He then introduced me to his minister, another Tom, and I introduced Nick as my partner. The conversation took an awkward turn into silence.

Suddenly I was nervous. Not necessarily for preaching, but because there I was—a gay man with his gay partner inside an obviously straight church even though I knew my friend was a gay man. But Tom and his minister were kind and welcoming to us, as far as I could tell. There was no open hostility. Certainly, they had known I was gay when they invited me?

"Well," I said to Nick. "We are here!" He squeezed my hand as parishioners began filing in.

When it came time to speak, Pastor Tom asked my friend to introduce me, and he did the heavy lifting for me—he said I was a gay refugee, and that I would speak with them about why I came to America. The stage was set for me to come up and speak, so I got up with as much confidence as I could muster, smiling at the parishioners while trying not to shake from nerves. As I turned to face them all, their smiling faces looking back at me, I thought I would feel terrified, but I was suddenly proud. So proud, in fact, that I could stand there as a gay man and hold the mic, with no objection from the congregants.

I gave a sermon on God's love. In the beginning of my sermon, I started with Jesus as a son and servant of God, referring to John 3:17: *For God sent his Son into the world not to judge the world, but to save the world through him.* And why do we, followers of Christ, have to judge and separate ourselves, when the

Bible made it clear not to judge? I continued with further Bible readings, this time from Romans 15:7: *God has been so kind to us, and he accepted us because of Jesus.* So it is imperative for us to accept one another as God did and show love to a stranger.

I wanted to change their hearts, to believe that gay people like me and Tom could be welcomed into their community, too, just as we were—open, proud, gay men. I left the pulpit, the church in total silence. The pastor continued the service.

We did not wait around for the service to end—Nick had become uncomfortable as they started anointing with olive oil, the people around us praying. When he walked out of the church, I immediately followed him, but he reassured me that he was okay, so I returned for the end. But back in New York, Tom called me. Apparently, the parishioners were not pleased. He and his minister faced strong rebukes for inviting a gay person to preach. What values were they trying to promote to their children? the congregants asked. I was disheartened. "How is your pastor taking all of this?" I asked Tom.

"He's well-respected," Tom said. "He'll be fine. But I can't stay at that church," he said. How heartbroken I was to see my friend try and fail to repair his relationship with his church, like I had done, time and time again.

At this point I was done, I told Tom. Religion and I would have to part ways. To me, the church was the same everywhere I turned—they pretended to be open-minded and loving, but they were not; it was all practiced with caveats, and on their terms. Nick tried to comfort me.

"When I came out as a teenager," he said, "the church wasn't my community anymore. And that was okay."

But for me, religion meant so much to me growing up; I knew that wasn't true for Nick. He didn't have the connection I had. He had never been a minister, a preacher, or anything like it. But I'd come so far in my plight to be a free gay man that maybe it was finally time to give up on being a religious gay man, too.

That was, until the summer of 2018, when I discovered the Unitarian church offices at the United Nations. This was when I met Bruce Knotts, the director of their programs, a tall man with salt-and-pepper hair, thick eyebrows, and a large gray beard. I was introduced to him because of his interest in immigration and asylum seekers, and he offered me a position as a youth representative of the Unitarian Universalist Association Office at the United Nations. I joined the UN in organizing the civil society conference in August 2018, and was included as one of their speakers, encouraged by Bruce and the organizers to give closing remarks on my experiences as a gay immigrant. How different this was! To be invited to share *all* parts of my story, rather than to tiptoe around it. I felt newly liberated, accepted, and celebrated, even. Shortly after this, Bruce referred me to the Unitarian Church in Toronto, Canada, to share more.

I traveled to Toronto with Nicholas, and we were hosted by Richard and Margaret, an older couple, living in Toronto. They welcomed us graciously into their home, which was a shock for Nick and me—they were a straight couple who believed in God, but they treated us like they would treat anyone else. Their faith felt different to me; I knew they saw and accepted me, and my faith, for what I was. I remember Richard putting it bluntly: "It's the same for me—gay or straight." How radical this was to hear for one of the very first times—if not for the first time ever.

During the Sunday service, the reverend encouraged his parishioners to speak to Nick and me during coffee hour afterward. The service that day was for the dead, and people were asked to bring photographs of their loved ones who passed away. The altar was furnished with photographs and candlelight. The reverend spoke about how our loved ones are not really gone until they are forgotten. Nick, who lost his dad at a young age, acknowledged to me how important it was for him to come to grips with something so difficult and see others who mourned their loved ones.

We felt at home, no longer suffering from having the Bible and Jesus forced upon us. They talked about different cultures being welcomed, believers of all faiths, nonbelievers, and LGBTQ people such as us. We were able to hold hands in the church without fear or judgment. Nick must have seen how important this was to me—saw something shifting within me that perhaps I couldn't even identify myself yet—and after the service he asked the reverend for the name of a Unitarian church in New York. I was shocked because Nick had never liked the idea of going to church on Sunday, but for me, he said we should at least go and see how it felt.

In New York the church we went to was on the Upper West Side. We arrived and I felt hesitant, still burnt-out by all my previous attempts at seeking inclusion. When we arrived, the building looked like any other Anglican church I grew up attending—but there was a stark difference: a rainbow flag flew outside the old stone walls, greeting us as we arrived. I had never seen—never dreamed of!—anything like this before. With Nick by my side, we entered and were greeted with smiles and welcomes as we found our seats.

We sat together, and I bravely held my boyfriend's hand in the pews. The service started with their creed: whomever you are, whomever you love, you are welcomed here. How radical to feel comfortable in a church? At the end of the service, we were greeted by Reverend Schuyler. "I hope you felt at home here," he said with a smile, and wished us a blissful week. On the way out, I noticed their Sunday bulletin had announcements about social justice issues they supported, such as LGBTQ rights, immigration, racial equality, and voting rights.

Returning to a Unitarian church helped me reconcile my understanding of religion. It helped me see that I can still believe in an omnipresent being. I can still believe in the commandments of loving God and thy neighbor, even if I've felt the church hasn't always practiced what it preached. I had been ashamed to call myself a Christian because of the harm Christianity brought unto me and my community. But the Unitarian way is guided by a philosophy of doing no harm. I have come to find a corner of Christianity that takes both my faith and my identity seriously—not in opposition to one another.

Even today, I still consider myself a preacher. But I have found a different gospel: a gospel of acceptance, not punishment; a gospel of love for one another and not hate. My faith as an adult, as a gay man, has shifted from the faith I had as a boy in Nigeria. I now know my faith can co-exist with identity; it does not have to be in a church. My faith is now situated in humanity. If I didn't have faith that people could change for the better, I would not be an activist.

CHAPTER SIX

The Courage to Lead around the World

I had $126 in my pocket, as recorded by immigration customs services when I arrived at JFK in 2016. For immigrants, the opportunity to live in America comes with its own price tag: the community you left back home has expectations for you to advocate and make their struggles known. In April 2018, I was given the opportunity to do that. When I joined the RDJ Refugee Shelter in Harlem, I was the second full-time director to walk through its doors. We had grant funding to last us for nine months; myself, one other employee named William Brown, and a handful of volunteers would have to find a way to organize and sustain the shelter. There were so many challenges laid out before me, but I didn't want anyone to have to face the struggles I had faced upon arriving in America: homelessness, anxiety, feelings of being lost, and of not having a community. So if I wasn't the best fit to run this center, then who? It became my mission to make sure no other LGBTQ refugees had to turn to sleeping on the streets of New York or be faced with a dilemma of being exploited sexually for a place to rest their head at night.

On my first day of working as the director, I traveled to Harlem from Sunnyside, Queens, to see the shelter I would be inheriting. Upon arriving, I entered through St. Mary's church as I had done during my interview. The church is one of the oldest buildings in Harlem and resembled the cathedral I had attended as a child. I walked through the gigantic space with its high ceilings and stained glass, and then followed a long staircase down into the basement where the refugees, asylum seekers, and displaced people slept. I couldn't believe my eyes—the ceiling was crumbling, the walls had cracks, and rodents roamed around. The only difference between this place and the detention center was the lack of cells and locks on the door. I had work to do—and I was excited to get the ball rolling. The appearance of the space dampened my spirit; I felt like the burning fire lost some of its energy, but not all of it.

On my first day of work, I was given a desk and computer to be shared with the church, and they were kept locked up in a cupboard to prevent theft. The more I walked around, the harsher the reality of the situation became. I was introduced to four clients that were currently living in the shelter: Luckner from Haiti; Arthur from Angola; and Kelly, who had fled from Jamaica to go to school and had come out as gay. He could not return to Jamaica because of the country's harsh treatment of queer folks, and after coming out, his family stopped financing his education. The last resident was a man named Dexter from Guyana, who had fled to America with the same expectations as me.

Dexter came to the RDJ shelter by way of the New York City rescue shelter, which was first come, first served every night. I was glad he had found us, but it was devastating to hear how horrible the process had been—which I could relate to.

In my first week of working at the shelter, I got a call from Sally at First Friends with a referral. There was a newly released immigrant from Honduras, who was transgender and needed a place to go. We did have a spare bed, and though I was worried about taking on more clients while still getting my bearings, I was not going to allow a transgender asylum seeker being released from the detention center to sleep on the street.

A volunteer from First Friends arrived with the young woman—and to my surprise it was Jenny, whom I'd met back in the Elizabeth Detention Center. I recalled the other detainees calling her *maricón*, taunting her, threatening her, and I remember feeling so helpless, unable to comfort her in Spanish, or keep her safe. Of course I would help Jenny.

Jenny still spoke no English, and her Honduran Spanish made it difficult to speak to her, so a volunteer offered to be a translator between us as she transitioned to our shelter.

Arthur, Luckner, Dexter, and Kelly were very welcoming to her. Jenny used a translator on her phone to help make conversation. I was glad they could communicate, even if just a little bit—but I still had to deal with language and cultural barriers, managing their cases, fundraising for the organization, providing them food, transporting them as necessary. There was a lot to manage—it was around then that I had begun seeing Nick, who was constantly amazed by my workload. I often worked seventy-hour weeks in those early days, and I explained to Nick that it was my responsibility, and the least I could do. We didn't have enough volunteers to work at the shelter, so some nights I would sleep there, covering the evening shift.

The nights I spent in the shelter were spent preparing food. I shared with them stories about my coming to America, and they shared their stories with me. It began to feel like we were building a family—which, at that point, I desperately needed. I knew from my own mental health struggles—feeling isolated and rejected as I arrived in America, dealing with the trauma of displacement and finding my feet—that it was imperative to find mental health support for the shelter guests. I took their stories and my concerns for them home with me—I worried about their health and well-being and became obsessed with the difficulties of our shared situations. But that also kept me driven to fight for them and for myself.

The job never stopped, really, even outside those seventy-hour work weeks. On one of my lunch dates with Nick, I received a call from William—one of the shelter guests had to be taken to the hospital. We ended the date abruptly and he drove me to the shelter to see what was happening. It turns out it was Jenny—she had been attacked, targeted for being transgender, while out on the streets in Harlem.

She was in the police precinct, across the street from our shelter, with the church rector. When I arrived, the rector left, and I had to stay with Jenny to make sure she was okay. I was not equipped to handle hate crime against a transgender immigrant; she looked battered. Nick, who had come with me, stroked my back. "Are you okay?" he whispered.

"I'm okay," I said. I did not want Jenny to sense my fear. But I felt I had failed her again—I couldn't protect her in the detention center, and here she was being attacked while under my care. It was that day that I realized my job would become my life. This work would have to extend beyond sitting quietly in my office writing grants all day. In order to fix the system, I would have to work outside it—I would have spoken up about the crisis LGBTQ asylum seekers and migrants face in America. This was during the summer of 2018, when the Trump administration's vitriolic immigration policies were at their peak, with the separation of families policy at our borders becoming the center of a heated national conversation. It seemed, perhaps, America was ready to listen.

In some ways, it was helpful to have immigration become the topic of conversation again—we received a renewed grant from a major funder; I was introduced to a new donor who organized a fundraiser for us; and throughout the summer, RDJ would garner plenty of media attention. But in those early days, I was responsible for almost everything—and I would listen to each newcomer's story, feeling our shared pain.

The administrative work kept getting delayed by new arrivals—I would try to finish a grant only to find someone wandering into the shelter with their bag in tow. On one particular day, a man wandered in with a familiar look of hopelessness on his face.

"Where are you from?" I asked.

"My name is John. I am from Jamaica, and an asylum seeker," he replied.

Already knowing the answer, I asked, "Welcome, John—are you hungry?"

"Yes," he replied with wide eyes. I kept snacks in the office and offered him something to eat. "Now, why don't you tell me your story?"

John found the shelter on Google. He was staying with his brother in the Bronx, but he had recently come out to his brother as gay. That was the final straw—he was told to leave. John slept on the train for some days; having no identification meant he couldn't access the city's shelters (a policy that changed in mid-2019 after tireless advocacy). He was doubly afraid because of his precarious immigration status. I smiled and offered him a tour.

The demand for space in our shelter was growing, but we were under-resourced—and my experience, energy, and mental health were sacrificed every day to support the asylees. It wasn't all that long ago that I could have found myself wandering into this same shelter with my backpack, my uncertainties. Yet here I was.

A question I had to ask myself constantly in my early days running the shelter was: What kind of country do we want to be going forward? I now had some power in shaping the answer to that question. I had always known America to be a beacon of hope to the world—but I saw firsthand that this wasn't true for immigrants. I knew the people who came to our shelter in search of a warm bed, hot soup, and socks for their feet—even if they'd sleep in the rusty basement of a church. I knew them because I was them. I knew they did not pose danger—the danger was what we fled.

My work as the director would not have been possible alone. I had support from Americans that I never expected. In nine months, my salary would run dry, the shelter would close, and we couldn't sustain ourselves only on grants. There was also the part-time staff to pay, and expenses for the shelter to run. We had to buy new beds, MetroCards for the shelter guests to attend appointments in court, ESL classes, and job training. Again, what sustained us was the goodwill of strangers—people donated suits or time to help update someone's résumé. There were more lighthearted field trips, too, like taking the shelter guests to the Statue of Liberty for the first time.

During the holidays, I organized the first Christmas party. Holidays were always the most difficult time for me, and I wanted to give them something to celebrate. Christmas in New York can be cold and isolating for people without a family. I was their family, so they were mine. I bought a tree and invited some volunteers who were available, to bring some gifts. Nick and I prepared some food, and I invited a few friends of mine, like Kent, my lawyer friend who had helped at my asylum trial.

We all gathered in the church and lit the tree. About eleven volunteers came with gifts and mingled with the shelter guests new and old. We celebrated like a family together, all dining on food from different cultures represented by each guest, a beautiful potluck. Walking home with Nick that evening, I felt fulfilled. Suddenly, my life was taking shape—I had a boyfriend who cared about me, and work I cared about, but I also felt, for the first time, like I had a family. My first Christmas in America, I spent behind bars at the detention center. Now, I had a life full of people whom I cared about, and who cared about me.

* * *

At the turn of 2019, we had more finances than I had expected from my grant work and donations, so I began renovating the space. I repaired the constant leak we had when it rained, which usually flooded the basement. We fixed the space heaters and repaired holes where a draft would blow in, and we hired an exterminator. Though these upgrades would improve the quality of life for the shelter guests, there was an ulterior motive. We needed to expand—and it would not be possible without more money, and more support. My friend Kent knew I had no resources to run a big operation like the shelter and that I was struggling. He offered to introduce me to his acquaintance Kevin Jennings, the president of the Tenement Museum in downtown Manhattan at the time, now the CEO of Lambda Legal. After our repairs, I invited Kevin to see the place.

Kevin arrived, an unimposing man with salt-and-pepper hair and cherry-colored cheeks. He was extremely well-mannered and greeted me with his polite Southern drawl. When he came inside the shelter, he was shocked. "People really live here?" he asked. Yes, I assured him. While we toured the space, I told him more about myself, sharing my story with him. Either moved or seeing a good opportunity, or both, he agreed to organize a fundraiser. His efforts could have helped us greatly, but I was still overwhelmed by the duties and responsibilities I handled daily. My one-year anniversary of running the shelter was approaching, and I knew something had to change.

My intention in starting this position was not to be the director of a social service organization; I believed the organization was a vehicle for me to create awareness and advocate for favorable policies for LGBTQ asylum seekers and refugees. I was contacted in February by the communication director of NowThis; they were looking to highlight immigration equality stories. I took the offer to share my story with the outlet, and so their director came to the office and put together a story about me and the shelter. On March 19, 2019, our first major press interview ran. It was a video featuring Jenny and me, speaking about our experiences.

Kevin and I used the video as part of our fundraiser narrative. We set a May date for the fundraiser. In March, I did an interview with the *Nation*, which ran that same month, building momentum about the narrative of LGBTQ asylum seekers in New York. By the time the fundraiser arrived, we had plenty of ammunition to lure in Kevin's amazing network. I met a reporter from NBC New York who did a story about the shelter for Pride month. I also met three big, future donors, one of whom was the late Henry van Ameringen, a gay philanthropist and icon, who, like Kevin, was a lifesaver.

We were finally gaining notoriety. We could up our bed count to ten, and I would be able to hire a full-time case manager to help transition folks into the shelter more seamlessly. I could point my time and energy elsewhere, to the forefront of the fight for LGBTQ asylum seekers in New York. In 2019 I was among the activists that organized the countermarch during the New York City Pride Parade. We retraced the original route of the first Pride march from Washington Square to Central Park. I began speaking at rallies and protests about the plights of LGBTQ asylum seekers. My name became synonymous with LGBTQ asylum seekers in New York.

In the summer of 2019, I decided to go on the journey to register the organization as a 501(c)(3), which would mean having a board of directors, bylaws, and accounting that was separate from the church we were based out of. At a fundraiser that summer, I met Matt Fischbein, a senior partner for Debevoise and Plimpton, the law firm that represented me in my asylum hearings. I told him more about my journey and asked for his help to register the organization as a nonprofit.

"Of course," he said, agreeing right there on the spot. The firm assigned us two lawyers: Richard, a corporate lawyer (also worked on my asylum case), and Ben, a tax lawyer. They would be our guide through the process, all pro bono. After a series of meetings—working with the church, the lawyers, and coming to agreements about the board of directors—we were dubbed the WANA Community Resource Center (or We Are Not Afraid). The organization was moving in a right direction, but there was no time to celebrate. All I was looking toward was the future and the possibility of raising more.

To organize dinners and events in New York was expensive, so I always had to be resourceful. For our big upcoming fundraiser, the first gala we ever arranged as an organization, the banquet hall was donated by Columbia University faculty through our donors, the food was paid for by corporate donors, and even Nick asked his organization to sponsor the event. The event was a success—despite accidentally scheduling the event on a major Jewish holiday and receiving pressure to reschedule—and a few days after the event we went ahead and submitted our registration as a tax-exempt organization with the IRS.

At the end of 2019, we also expanded our services to serve asylum seekers who did not live in our shelter but needed case management assistance. The vision of our work expanded to be a safe space for asylum seekers and provide food and nourishment to people experiencing hunger in Harlem. We provided hot meals to homeless people on the street, and whatever support we could offer to those who came into our shelter.

The year ended with the news of Dexter winning his asylum case after months of waiting for a hearing. We were overjoyed—but he could not stay with us now that he was granted asylum. This was another part of our job—to help him secure housing with our partner organization Seafarers International House.

Early one morning in the fall of 2018, I rushed out of my apartment to get to my office before my clients started pouring in. Though my office is just a few hundred feet from the subway on 126th Street, I got caught in a torrential rainfall without an umbrella. I had lived here for a while now, but I somehow always forget an umbrella. I ran out of the train station, weaving through the crowd of people, and I got to the shelter, soaked. Though at first I was anxious walking through the shelter and the church, by then it had become a sanctuary that relaxed me—my home away from home.

I turned on the space heater in my office and began doing some paperwork, when Dexter walked into the office. He laughed at me for not knowing it was going to rain. After Dexter migrated from Guyana, his mother had died, due to a lack of emergency response when she was critically ill. He could not return to his country for her funeral, as he was seeking protection in America.

He pronounced my name that morning with a long stretch, "Edafeeeeee!"

I turned from my desk: "Dexter, I don't have time, say what you want to say. I have a busy day."

Dexter broke the happy news. "I just graduated as an EMT today!"

I stopped what I was doing and stood to hug him tightly, despite my wet clothes. As he pulled away, he laughed a sigh of relief. We both knew that after many months of working, he would now have a job and be able to fend for himself. New York City and America had become a home to Dexter, as it had become a home for me.

There was no other befitting way to end the year than to celebrate one of my clients who would begin his own work impacting the lives of New Yorkers. This was exactly how the shelter should work—and though I was often overworked, tired, and distressed from the daily ins and outs of all I witnessed, I was proud. I was happy. I was helping people. We have since had 265 people spend the night under our roof, and have helped over two thousand asylum seekers who have crossed our threshold asking for help with lawyers, health care access, work authorization forms, and even those who come simply on a Friday night to watch a movie, have warm soup, and enjoy conversation with others who know what they've been through.

Working as the director of a refugee shelter has given my life renewed meaning and a sense of direction, but it continues to be challenging work. In December 2019, I organized my second

Christmas party for the shelter. Volunteers agreed to join us in a potluck of gifts and food. We had more RSVP volunteers than people living in our shelter. The day of, I came early and made coffee. We discussed our lives in this country as newly migrated asylum seekers and asylees. This year, I was more aware of the challenges these people faced, but their stories hit me no matter how many times I'd heard similar tales—they missed their families; they were disappointed that America wasn't more welcoming. I understood all too well. "I did not know I would be sleeping in the basement of a church when I arrived in America," Mohammed, a journalist from Iran, remarked.

"The basement is a lot better off than this time last year," I told him.

Some of the asylum seekers were down, it being a holiday, so I spent the early hours cheering them up while we strung lights around the center and volunteers began dropping gifts off under our modest tree. We ate food based on recipes selected by the asylees, with meals from Ethiopia, Guyana, Syria, and elsewhere.

It was a lovely night of sharing food and unboxing presents—winter jackets, blankets, hot chocolate packs. Walking home that evening, I thought of my own family, and how alone I still felt in America. But I had pressed on before, and I would do so again. Early in 2020, following our celebration, five of those asylum seekers moved into their first apartments. Things started to click into place for me—building family in a new country was difficult, but it was happening, for myself and those I helped, slowly but surely. I wasn't doing this so that I would personally stop becoming the target for others' hatred. I fought because of the sense of refuge it gave to me as someone encountering this hate;

and because I knew I was helping inspire thousands of younger people who witnessed the strength drawn from my leadership. I was doing my small part in making America a leader in helping others, at home and around the world. I mustered the courage to fight, despite the backlash I faced, because my life has to be a refuge for others; my hope is that we will all consider becoming a refuge for people who have a thirst for freedom.

Nick's thirtieth birthday presented us an opportunity to travel. I didn't usually take vacations, as there was always so much work to do, but I felt I had earned some time for celebration. I insisted we take a break between Valentine's Day and Nick's birthday, and so we spent the weekend in Costa Rica. It was a very lovely short squeeze, but fun. I even took a photo album of the trip, because we went to see an active volcano and swam in warm springs.

Upon returning, I had just placed my luggage on the bed when my phone rang. It was William; his usual cheery tone was gone.

"Good evening, Edafe," he began quietly. "I just wanted to let you know we have another emergency at the shelter, and we need to talk."

"Can it wait until the morning?" I asked. In the past, William had taken some non-emergency issues out of context.

Sure, he told me, somewhat hesitantly.

The next morning, I barely had a chance to turn on my computer before William appeared. "Edafe," he began. "We received a client, Jose, who was scheduled to come into the shelter from the detention center two days ago. Last night, I got a call from another guest at the shelter that he was very sick and needed to be taken to the hospital. When I arrived, his lawyer and case manager had rushed him to Mount Sinai on 147th Street," he told me breathlessly. "When I asked why, they did not give me a clear nor direct message—because they needed to speak with you, the director. He has a fluctuation in his sugar level and a fever. That's all I know."

I listened in stunned silence, afraid that the worst might be true. "Now that you are here, I would like you to go see him or give me a letter with your signature that I am permitted to see him." I quickly signed the letter and permitted him to represent me so I could read through my emails.

Without any other word, William left. As he paced out of the room, I felt something was off, but I continued to read through my emails and helped the other guest at the shelter who needed my attention. I worked late into the evening, hearing no more from William.

Three days later, the day Jose was supposedly scheduled to be discharged from the hospital, I called the clinic to inform them I would be coming by noon to pick him up. The receptionist replied, "The doctor left a note. Should I read it for you?"

"Sure," I replied.

" 'We are deeply sorry to inform his friends and family that Jose died last night; we noticed during our routine check in the wee hours of the morning.' "

I sat silently on the phone, not a word could come out of my mouth. The nurse continually asked, "Hello, sir? Are you there? Are you there?"

"Yes," I finally replied. "I will inform his family. Thank you."

I sat on the floor, crying. I did not know who to call or what else to do. I was in a state of shock. Jose sounded lively when he arrived, and William said that he was excited to get his life going, to look for a job. Now he was no more. The immigration detention center where he was kept did not give him the care he needed, and though he was released, he still died due to negligence of care.

I have experienced different types of displacement: people have walked into our doors with different sorts of stories; each new guest peeling back the wounds that are not fully healed, reminding me of the perils of surviving in America as an asylum seeker. But losing Jose, a fellow gay refugee, felt more urgent. It gave me a new mission—that the stories of people seeking freedom should be told.

As fulfilling as I find my work with LGBTQ refugees and asylum seekers at the shelter, I have also struggled with the idea of a refugee with lived experience leading this movement.

It took me quite some time to realize I'd never formally done anything to reckon with my past. I had run away from it, buried it, and replaced it with a new, wonderful life. But it was, and will always be, a part of me. I have scars on my body from the mob that attacked me in Nigeria to prove this, to remind me.

Eventually, I sought out a therapist, which led me to the Bellevue Program for Survivors of Torture in downtown New York, where my recovery began. They helped me realize that my work at RDJ—as important as it has always been to me—was also not allowing me to relive my own trauma. Each new story that came with someone arriving on our steps reopened the wounds of my own arrival. I would lie awake, unable to sleep, rethinking the scenario of how I could have helped the client that got deported, how I could have helped the client that died.

When I started therapy, I was overwhelmed by the decisions in front of me—to continue a relationship with my family, which had become a matter of quid pro quo in as much that they would only acknowledge me as family if I sent them money. No money sent, no love in return. But my therapist helped me build a new form of relationship with myself and my family. In due time, my mother and sisters would come to accept my sexuality and my partner. My family would come to understand that I would never stop being gay. Still, each day brought new lessons in learning how to handle my anxiety, not letting my past control my future.

It begs on me to call on LGBTQ Americans and allies of refugees to understand the struggle we face. As a refugee, it takes courage to stand up for what you believe in, because it often comes with great personal risk. That is why, through my work, I hope to implore others to stand and speak up beside me. During the summer of 2020, amid the peak of the coronavirus, there was a turn in the movement. More people began to understand the issues Black Americans face on a daily basis. This was encouraging, but it is a movement that I hope continues—that it does not die down. I would hope the empathy those have displayed in understanding race in this country may also extend to understanding the plight of immigrants, asylees, and displaced people.

In 2020, I stopped handling case management at the shelter, but I would visit regularly. On one occasion, I met a refugee named Duke, from Venezuela, who spoke English.

"What is your story, Duke?" I asked him as he strolled into my office that day.

"Do you have some time?" He sat, and I made him a cup of coffee from the new machine we had bought. He sighed. "What a relief, to drink coffee."

"So," I began, "tell me. Is America what you expected?"

Duke had stayed in Mexico for a year before gaining admission into the United States. He left his children and family back in 2015, when his journey began. He was part of the political movement in Venezuela, and due to subsequent riots he became a target by a gang. He knew that to be safe, he had to flee, with no money or form of support. He fled to Colombia, from there to Panama, and through the Darien jungle to Mexico. He slept at shelters and makeshift camps with horrible conditions, witnessed murders and terrible hardships of other immigrants, just to make it to the U.S. border. There, he was detained by immigration in San Jose. Due to the REMAIN in Mexico Act, he was returned to a makeshift camp. When the incoming Biden administration signed an executive order to repeal this act, Duke was able to reenter the United States—but with no place to stay at the Southern border, he was sent to New York by a group of volunteers from a nonprofit.

"This place is like a palace," he said, looking around my office. To him, that probably felt true after what he'd been through. Duke was good with numbers, he told me, and was hoping to get a job down on Wall Street.

Though it sounded harrowing, he told me this story fondly. He had made it, after all.

CHAPTER SEVEN

Risking It All for Freedom

Every day we are faced with choices: when to wake up, if we should shower, what we should eat for breakfast. We make big choices, too, about our purpose, our freedom, and our happiness. Only some of us will ever be faced with the choice to run for safety. These bold choices come with crippling fears—we could fail, we could be rejected. For a refugee, these considerations are not part of the equation. The choices we make are matters of life and death. Those life-and-death pushes are sometimes what drive us—not only toward freedom, but toward a shameless pursuit of our dreams, even if that means abandoning everything and everyone we know in the process.

This journey to America as an asylum seeker has taught me about resilience, faith, and community. I have met new people, kind and compassionate friends along the way. I have faced danger and hardship, but nevertheless, I am alive. I am alive and better off than I was in my homeland, but the feeling of home has never left me. It's easy to see in hindsight how you take those around you for granted. I wonder now where so many of my childhood friends are, like Gloria. My family and I never said *I love you* much; how I wish I could tell them, to their faces, that I love them. I miss my mother especially, watching her dance on the veranda while local drug sellers would pass by singing. I miss her jollof rice that she would make on Christmas Day. I miss the scolding clucks of my aunts. I miss seeing my sisters' children grow up. I have missed so much I never even knew—what it was like to wrap up cute gifts for my nieces and nephews on their birthdays, reading them stories well past their bedtimes.

Most of the times I think about my close family members, whom I might never get to meet again. In early 2021, I received a call that my father was ill. I was not sure he would make it out of the hospital, and I could not go to visit him. The only thing I could do was offer support in America. The only reason I could not do more was because of my status as a refugee.

I found new friends and family in America and have never doubted that these people will be with me for the rest of my life.

That is the risk I took. Now I have to look on from a distance at my family back home in Nigeria while building something of my own here in the United States. But if you asked me if I would risk it all again to build this new life with the freedom to be myself, or to have stayed in a world where I was constantly afraid to be who I truly am, I would choose freedom every time.

You can love from a distance; we are faced with choices every day. For what happened in the past we can blame others, but for what will happen in the future we cannot blame anyone but ourselves. The small choices we make today will make up our life stories tomorrow.

Family can be the people you are born to, but if you are lucky like me, you get to pick a family of your choosing. I have places to go and people to celebrate holidays with. I have a big chosen family, and it keeps growing every day. I know who will walk me down the aisle when I get married. I now have a Jewish mother in Emily. And another mother in Dorothy. Flora is the younger sister I never had, and I attended her graduation in Boston. I have Kent, and Mrs. Ross, and Cristina. I have Sylvester. And I have countless others—friends and mentors—who have become my family. I was a stranger when they met me, but they welcomed me into their worlds without judgment of who I am.

I feel lucky enough to have taken risks, and to trust the universe with an open heart. I have so many reasons not to love, but I will not let that stop me.

The year I turned twenty-nine, I had a wish. I have never driven a car my entire life and I wanted to drive a car before I turned thirty. Nicholas drove me wherever I needed to go, but I didn't want to rely on him if I needed a car in the future. He agreed to teach me how to drive because he taught his little sister when she was seventeen. I had never sat in the driver's seat. "I really can't drive, you know," I said. And Nick laughed, not realizing I wasn't joking.

He took me to an empty high school parking lot, close to his sister's house on Long Island, and handed me the keys. I stared at him in the passenger's seat, not knowing what to do. He tried explaining, but it all escaped me. As soon as I turned the ignition, we started moving fast and I almost hit a garbage can before I found the brake. Then Nick realized I was serious; I *really* couldn't drive. It took me a while to be comfortable staying alone inside the car, but I was willing to learn. With Nick, my life has been learning. He taught me how to swim, took me to my first hockey game, took me snowmobiling. But I have also learned how to love, and to be loved, through him. My life with Nicholas has been worth every risk I took to be here.

I can vividly remember the first time I kissed Nick on the streets of Manhattan. It felt like a dream. He was the shy one, but I was in disbelief. Something so simple had never been in the realm of possibility in my old life. Before him, before my work with other refugees, I never understood unconditional love. Many people have loved me conditionally over the years—for what I would become, what I meant to our family, for my drive and passion. But with Nick, love has always felt unconditional—he loves me no matter who I become or where my passions lie.

The shock of losing everything I had made me refuse to accept the notion that someone would love me for who I am. This becomes a pattern, a defensive mechanism to shield yourself from harm. I have had to learn that going through difficulties presents opportunities for you to start again, to try *again*. Dexter, Jenny, and other asylum seekers I have worked with as the director of RDJ Refugee Shelter have constantly exemplified the idea of not giving up even when everything is working against your favor and it feels impossible to think of a new day.

Immigrants know how to fight when our backs are up against a wall. Most Americans can't relate—relatively, because Americans are afforded so many privileges. But what most Americans overlook is that someone in their family—their parents, their grandparents, their great-great-great-grandparents—had to sacrifice a great deal to come here, too.

It is almost five years to the day since I walked into the terminal at JFK, seeking asylum. These days, I live on the Upper West Side of Manhattan. I wake up early to make pumpkin-spiced flavored coffee and listen to podcasts before taking a morning walk in Central Park. I have a life now, a roof over my head, a gym membership, a job, a partner I love. I have won awards and recognition for my work; I have pursued a master's degree at New York University. By all accounts, I am succeeding—yet part of me will always miss my life in Nigeria.

During my morning walks in Central Park, I like to take deep breaths and listen to the sounds of New York waking up around me. My mind often travels back home—but I sometimes remind myself that here, where I stand today, is home now. And I must also remember that so little has changed in Nigeria—there are growing protests against police brutality, and the gay rights movement still struggles. Then there is guilt. How do I deserve this life, when thousands of people come to America and never find a place of their own?

Learning to embrace myself was not the easiest road to travel, but I would not have been able to tell this story if I did not learn how to embrace who I am. There have been as many downs as there have been ups. But I thrive because my story showed me who I am. I am a tough cookie; nothing can make me doubt the possibility of who I may become if I put my heart into it.

We are all on our own paths, and we all have something to offer. But if my journey has taught me anything, it's that we must choose love over hate, we must stand up for what is right, always, and fight for what we believe in. Follow your convictions and your intuition, and when you fail, know that you failed trying.

As a refugee, life could not be more palatable for me these days. I don't deny the privilege I have as someone who made it, one person out of the millions of people who try each year. For this reason, I have dedicated my life to fighting for global equality, and I want to call on you to do the same. We can make the world a better place, and that is the task we all have before us. To leave this world a little bit better than when we came in; you have your role to play in the larger scheme. When I was a child, people asked me what I wanted to become when I grew up. I always believed what my father and mother professed, even my grandma, Mrs. Alice—they all wanted me to become a doctor or a pastor or someone who impacted people's lives in a meaningful way.

No, I am not a medical doctor, neither am I a pastor, but I have become something, and someone. I have become a bridge builder. An advocate. A leader. I have become myself.

As an asylee, a refugee, I will never be the president of any country. Technically speaking, we don't even have citizenship of any country. That is why this book exists: to make you part of our country, to give you our stories, so you can help us make policies and build new realities that will enable us to participate in the world with you. We are displaced due to man-made policies, we fled when home was no longer safe, we became destitute in a foreign land, and all we ask for in return is your compassion.

To see us for who we are and to give us a genuine opportunity to build a life of our design.

In the last few years, I have been asked, "Where are you from?" I answer, "Nigeria." And then people tell me I am far away from home. But my response is always the same: this is home for me now. Home is not just where you feel safe and welcome. It is also about how you can make it feel safe and welcoming for others.

Acknowledgments

This book started with my mother, Mrs. Igho Akanusi; my grandmother, Mrs. Alice Akanusi; my aunt, Mrs. Grace Erhimona; and my partner, Nicholas Giglio. Many folks have been family to me, and it would not be a memoir if I did not mention a few.

Summer McKee and the team at Debevoise & Plimpton, Cristina Rodriquez-Hart, Kent Klindera, Dorothy Wetzel, Emily Kullman, Sally Pillay, Jeffrey Davis, and all the beautiful people I've met along my journey. John Wilkinson and the team at the Bellevue Program for Survivors of Torture, First Friends of NJ & NY, Immigration Equality, Eat Offbeat, William Brown, and the team at RDJ Refugee Shelter. And last but not least, Dr. Eric Cervini.

This book would not have been possible without the dedication of my editor, Zachary Knoll, and my agent, Daniel Lazar, at Writers House. Thank you for your vision of this work.

I cannot mention everyone in my life. But this book would not have been possible without all of you.

About the Author

Edafe Okporo was born in Warri, Nigeria. He migrated to the United States in 2016 as an asylum seeker and is now a refugee of the United States. Edafe is a global gay rights activist, the founder of Refuge America, and one of the country's most visible voices on the issue of displacement, leading an organization with a vision to provide a welcoming place for displaced LGBTQ people. He is a graduate of Enugu State University and the Stern School of Business at NYU.

Edafe is among the inaugural winners of the David Prize, which honors individuals with bold visions for creating a better and brighter New York City. He is also a Logo30 honoree. He lives in New York City.